A
Cape Cod
Seafood
Cookbook

A Cape Cod
SEAFOOD
Cookbook

Margaret Deeds Murphy

Drawings by Harold Durand White

PARNASSUS IMPRINTS
Orleans, Cape Cod

*Dedicated to my sister Dorothy
for her love and support
and to the Cape Cod Seafood Council
for their shared knowledge.*

Contents

A
Cape Cod
Seafood
Cookbook

Introduction

Cape Cod is as close to being an island surrounded by salt water as it could possibly be without being one. It wasn't always thus, as Cape Cod was connected directly to the rest of Massachusetts until 1914. In that year the Cape Cod Canal was finished, forming an inner water passage from points south to the New England coast.

The Cape sticks 65 miles out into the Atlantic Ocean. Along its 586-mile coastline fishermen catch the many varieties of fish for which the Cape is famous. The tidal rivers and harbors where clams, scallops, mussels, and oysters grow and are harvested also add their names to the fame of Cape Cod seafood, a bonus of great taste and distinction.

Because the Pilgrims settled permanently in Plymouth, Massachusetts, in 1620, we forget that Bartholomew Gosnold named the Cape back in 1602. The story is told that Gosnold, an English captain exploring the coast, first named the Cape Shoal Hope. After making a large catch of codfish, however, he changed Cape Shoal Hope to Cape Cod.

Codfish became such an important industry after the settlers made good that the Sacred Cod became the emblem of the Commonwealth of Massachusetts and hangs in the State House and other official buildings.

The recipes that follow have the taste of the Cape as well as a little flavor of Cape Cod history.

General Information on Seafood

All seafood is fragile and should be handled with great care from the time you buy it until it is cooked.

- First choose a fish market that is clean and sanitary. Fresh fish should not smell. If buying frozen fish, check for signs of its having been defrosted and refrozen. Do not buy it if you suspect this.
- Fish should be firm fleshed. A whole fish should have bright eyes that are not sunken into the head.

• Fish should be refrigerated at the market. During hot weather, if fish cannot be transported quickly from the fish market to the home refrigerator, ice a small cooler and put the fish in that to keep it cold.
• Two days is the maximum time fish should be refrigerated before being cooked. If it is not possible to cook fish promptly, freeze it in freezer paper or foil. (See Freezing Directions.) If using frozen seafood, always defrost in the refrigerator before cooking.

Not only is a wide variety of seafood available, it is also a most nutritious food. Seafood is a source of complete protein, meaning that its protein contains all the amino acids necessary for proper growth and repair of the body tissues. It is as good for you as the protein in meat, poultry, or cheese.

Fish is also a good source of B vitamins, which include thiamin, riboflavin, niacin, vitamin B_6, vitamin B_{12}, and pantothenic acid.

Minerals found in fish are iron, potassium, phosphorus, copper, iodine, manganese, cobalt, and other trace minerals necessary for good health.

Most fish is low in fat content. Fat content may be less than 1 percent, as in the cod family, or as much as 10 percent for salmon or mackerel. So, depending on what is added to fish when it is cooked, it can be extremely low in calories.

Seafood Nutrition

Fish 5.3 oz. raw edible portion	Percent protein	Percent fat	Calories per 5.3 oz.	Sodium mg.
Bluefish	19.2	3.3	203	88
Clams	11.0	1.7	95	383
Cod	17.4	0.5	114	136
Crab	15.7	2.7	124	499
Cusk	18.5	0.6	148	—
Flounder	18.1	1.4	133	183
Haddock	18.2	0.5	117	148
Hake	16.6	1.3	162	125
Halibut	18.7	4.3	180	236
Lobster	18.1	1.4	148	448
Mackerel	19.5	9.9	161	50

Fish 5.3 oz. raw edible portion	Percent protein	Percent fat	Calories per 5.3 oz.	Sodium mg.
Monkfish	17.6	9.5	236	151
Mussels	11.9	1.4	117	324
Ocean perch	14.5	0.7	138	—
Ocean catfish	17.6	2.8	233	145
Oysters	8.5	1.8	103	—
Pollock	19.7	1.3	138	—
Salmon	19.9	9.3	247	115
Scallop	14.6	0.7	118	246
Shrimp	18.6	1.6	136	201
Swordfish	19.4	4.4	178	154
Sole	16.9	1.4	126	141
Shark, mako	17.0	12.2	269	—
Tautog	—	—	113	—
Tuna	24.7	5.1	254	95
Whiting	18.9	1.3	136	76

Source: National Marine Fisheries

Market Forms of Fresh Fish

When you are purchasing fish it is helpful to know the various forms in which it comes.

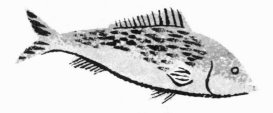

Whole: Fish as they come from the water. Before cooking, the fish must be scaled and eviscerated — usually the head, tail, and fins are removed. The fish may then be cooked, filleted, or cut into steaks or chunks.

Dressed: Fish with scales and entrails removed. Usually the head, tail, and fins are also removed. The fish may then be cooked, filleted, or cut into steaks or chunks. The smaller size fish are called pan-dressed and are ready to cook as purchased.

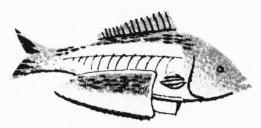

Fillets: Fillets are the sides of the fish cut lengthwise away from the backbone. They are ready to cook as purchased. A fillet cut from one side of a fish is called a *single fillet*. This is the type most generally available on the market. The fillets may or may not be skinless. *Butterfly fillets* are the two sides of the fish cut lengthwise away from the backbone and held together by the uncut flesh and skin of the belly.

Steaks: Steaks are cross-section slices from large dressed fish, cut ⅝ to 1 inch thick. A cross section of the backbone is the only bone in a steak. They are ready to cook as purchased.

Chunks: Chunks are cross sections of large dressed fish. A cross section of the backbone is the only bone in a chunk. They are ready to cook as purchased.

When you are buying fish, how much should be purchased for each person to be served? The following are guidelines for the different cuts in which fish can be purchased. These are based on adult appetites.

Whole fish	¾ pound per person
Dressed or pan dressed	½ pound per person
Fillets or steak	⅓ to ½ pound
Chunks	⅓ to ½ pound

Fish Seasons

Legend:
- ■ Plentiful
- ▨ Available
- ░ Scarce

	January	February	March	April	May	June	July	August	September	October	November	December
Cod												
Haddock												
Pollock												
Sole or flounder												
Whiting												
Ocean perch												
Mackerel												
Ocean scallops												
Bay scallops												
Lobster												
Maine shrimp												
Ocean catfish												
Cusk												
Hake												
Eel												
Squid												
Striped bass												
Bluefish												
Mako shark												
Tautog												
Dogfish												
Swordfish												

Cooking Fish

There are six basic ways in which fish can be cooked. But the most important thing of all is to remember that fish *must not be overcooked.* Directions that say "until fish can be easily flaked with a fork" mean just that. Fish still undercooked will have a translucent appearance and the fork will not be able to separate the flakes. Fish that is overcooked becomes hard and the fork has difficulty penetrating the flesh to flake the fish.

When a recipe says "cook 8 minutes or until fish flakes with a fork," I recommend that you test it at 7 minutes just in case your range is a little different from that of the person who gave you the recipe. If it needs the extra minute you will know. A self-cleaning oven is better insulated and has a tendency to be a little hotter and certainly hold the heat longer than a non-self-cleaner.

These are the basic ways to cook fish.

Baking

Fish should be baked at 375° or 400° F. Allow 10 minutes per inch of thickness, measuring at the thickest part.

Broiling

This method depends on the thickness of the fish and the distance from the source of heat. A good rule is to broil 4 inches from the source of heat. For thin fillets, 5 to 8 minutes will cook the fish. Do not turn. Pieces over 1 inch thick should be turned once and can take up to 15 minutes total time.

Frying

Heat vegetable oil to 375° F for frying fish. At least 2 inches of oil are necessary, and the fish will probably have to be turned to brown both sides. A 375° F temperature browns the outer crust of the fish, sealing in the juices. Depending on the size of the pieces being fried, it should take from 3 to 5 minutes for them to reach golden brown.

Sauteing

Sauteing means cooking in a skillet with just enough butter, margarine, or oil to keep the fish from sticking. Use medium high heat and carefully turn the fish with a spatula to brown both sides. Again, the thickness of the fillets will control the time. Thin fillets will probably require a total of 5 minutes, thicker ones 8 minutes. The fillets may be dipped in flour or crumbs before sauteing, if one desires.

Poaching

Poached fish is cooked in liquid below the boiling point. Combine enough liquid to cover the fish — water or water plus dry white wine — with onion slices, parsley, celery leaves, peppercorns, and any other herbs you wish to use. Bring to a boil and simmer, covered, for 15 to 20 minutes. Add fish and cook below boiling point 10 minutes per inch thickness. Strain stock after fish is cooked, and if the stock is not to be used in the recipe, freeze it. It can be used again for poaching or as liquid in a fish soup or sauce. If you are poaching a whole fish but do not have a fish poacher (which is a relatively expensive piece of equipment), use a large flat pan and wrap the fish in cheesecloth to make it easier to remove from the liquid without breakage.

Steaming

Steamed fish is cooked on a rack over boiling water in a covered pan until it flakes easily. Again, the length of time will depend on the thickness of the fillets. Check at the end of 8 minutes. Steamed fish can be used for salad or served plain or with sauce.

Microwave

Fish cooks very well in the microwave oven. Remember that microwave cooking is rapid; follow the timing and power directions to the Tee. You may want to add a little color to the appearance of the fish with toasted crumbs, paprika, chopped parsley, and/or herbs when it is cooked.

Interchanging Fish

Interchanging fish in recipes can be done with great success.

- Cod, haddock, pollock, hake, cusk, ocean catfish, ocean perch, and halibut are all white-fleshed fish and can be used interchangeably.
- Mako shark, salmon, tuna fish, and swordfish are more fatty fish and can be used interchangeably in recipes.
- Flounder and sole fillets substitute for each other.
- Tautog and dogfish are fish with a coarse texture and could be used

in scallop recipes, though of course they cannot be considered substitutes for scallops.

More Fish Tales

• Rub lemon juice over your fingers before handling fish so that the odor does not cling to your hands.
• Use leftover cooked fish for salads, casseroles, or creamed fish. Remove skin and bones and flake fish.
• Generous amounts of lemon or lime juice squeezed on fish several hours before cooking enhance the flavor.

Appetizers

Seafood is without peer as an appetizer, whether you add a little garnish or serve the seafood simply. Take the dip made with cream cheese and clams. That recipe has been around for at least 30 years and its popularity has extended over generations of Americans.

Most seafood as such is low in calories. It is the ingredients added to it in the recipe, such as mayonnaise, butter, or cooking oil, that crank up the calorie content. If you are counting calories, steamed mussels, raw oysters, or clams served with a squeeze of lemon juice make wonderful appetizers at about 10 calories each.

When you are preparing cold seafood appetizers it is wise to use several small platters. Keep all but the one being served in the refrigerator. As one platter empties, bring a new one. This keeps the food fresh and appealing.

Garnish platters with radish roses, parsley, watercress, or lemon slices or wedges to add to the festive look of the platter of food.

If you are having a large party, avoid soupy dips. It is too easy for them to end up in drips on the rug.

To have fun at your own party, use recipes that can be prepared in advance as much as possible.

* * *

Chef Pepper's Cocktail Fish Cakes

Among my first memories of the Cape were small hot fish cakes served at the witching hour. After a day in the sand and sun they were ambrosia.

2 medium potatoes
½ pound boneless cod or other white fish
Dash Tabasco sauce
4 tablespoons grated Parmesan cheese
3 tablespoons cream cheese
1 packet instant chicken bouillon
1 teaspoon dried onion
Milk (if needed)
1 egg, beaten
2 tablespoons water
1 cup (about) dry bread crumbs
2 tablespoons butter

Peel and quarter potatoes. Cook in boiling water until almost tender. Add fish and continue to cook until potatoes are tender and fish flakes easily. Drain well and beat potatoes and codfish together until blended. Add Tabasco, cheeses, bouillon, and dried onion and mix well. If mixture is dry beat in a small amount of milk. Shape into 16 small cakes. Mix egg and water. Dip cakes in egg and then in bread crumbs. Heat butter in skillet and fry cakes until lightly browned on both sides. Makes 16. Serve hot with picks.

Tasty Fish Dip

Serve this dip in your prettiest bowl and win compliments.

½ pound smoked bluefish or smoked haddock (finnan haddie)
1 cup dairy sour cream
2 tablespoons lemon juice
2 teaspoons chopped chives
1 teaspoon grated onion
¼ teaspoon dried rosemary, crushed
½ teaspoon coarsely ground pepper
Assorted crackers or raw vegetables

Poach fish in water for 5 to 7 minutes. Cool.

Remove skin and any bones from fish and flake finely. Combine with all remaining ingredients except crackers or vegetables. Mix lightly to blend. Chill well in a covered container, several hours or overnight. If you desire, garnish with paprika or chopped fresh parsley. Serve with crackers or vegetables. Makes 1¾ cups.

Fish Puffs

This recipe is more easily made in a food processor, but directions for making without a food processor are also given.

    ½ cup butter or margarine
    1 cup boiling beer
    1 cup all-purpose flour
    4 eggs
    1¼ cups shredded smoked haddock (finnan haddie)

Combine butter and boiling beer in a saucepan over low heat. When butter is melted add flour all at once and stir very hard until mixture forms a ball and leaves sides of pan. Allow mixture to cool 5 minutes.

Put mixture into processor bowl with steel blade. Add eggs one at a time through the chute, processing after each addition. When all the eggs have been added, the dough should be firm enough to hold its shape when dropped from a spoon. Add fish and process until well blended.

Or to prepare without a food processor, remove cooked mixture from heat and beat eggs in one at a time with a wooden spoon or electric mixer, beating well after each addition. Chop fish finely and beat into batter.

Drop by teaspoons on a greased baking sheet and bake at 400° F for 20 to 25 minutes or until lightly browned. Cool on rack. Makes about 60. May be served hot or cold.

Fish puffs may be frozen and will keep up to 2 weeks; defrost to serve. The batter may also be frozen for up to 2 weeks. Defrost and bake as directed.

Eel Party Mold

This pretty and tasty mold is perfect for a buffet or cocktail party.

1½ pounds eel
½ pound green shrimp, peeled and cleaned
1 medium onion, sliced
6 peppercorns
2 bay leaves
½ teaspoon salt
1 envelope unflavored gelatin
½ cup cold water
2 tablespoons vinegar
2 hard-cooked eggs, cut in wedges
1 cup cooked tiny peas
Parsley
Mayonnaise

Skin and clean eel (see instructions in Entrees) and cut into 1-inch pieces. Remove backbone. Place eel and shrimp in a saucepan and add water to cover. Add onions, peppercorns, bay leaves, and salt. Bring to just below boiling and poach 3 to 4 minutes. Remove eel and shrimp from liquid; strain liquid and reserve.

Soften gelatin in ½ cup cold water. If reserved eel liquid is no longer hot, bring back to simmer, then remove from heat. (There should be about 1½ cups.) Add gelatin and vinegar to liquid and stir until gelatin is dissolved. Chill in refrigerator until mixture begins to have texture of raw egg white. Arrange shrimp in bottom of a rinsed 1½-quart ring mold. With a spoon pour about ¼ of gelatin over shrimp. Chill until set. Keep remainder of gelatin at room temperature. Arrange eel pieces and eggs over shrimp and spoon half of remaining gelatin over eel and eggs. Chill until set.

Spoon peas over eel and add remaining gelatin. Chill for several hours or until firm.

To serve, unmold on platter and garnish with parsley sprigs. If you desire, mayonnaise may be served with mold.

· MAKO SHARK ·

Mako shark has become extremely popular over the past few years. It is often chosen as a less expensive substitute for swordfish, having much the same texture and flavor. Buy it at a fish market where you know it will be fresh.

Potted Mako

This party recipe will please everyone. It makes a delightful spread with a new kind of flavor.

2 pounds Mako shark
6 tablespoons butter or margarine, softened
1 tablespoon anchovy paste
½ teaspoon ground nutmeg
⅛ teaspoon Tabasco sauce
2 tablespoons lemon juice

Spread Mako with 2 tablespoons butter and broil 4 inches from source of heat 6 to 8 minutes, turning if Mako is more than 1 inch thick. The fish should be just done when flaked with a fork, but not dried out. Cool and remove skin and bones. Cut fish into small squares and blend in food processor with steel blade until fish is as fine as possible. Gradually add the rest of the butter and the other remaining ingredients, processing until well blended. Spoon into a 3-cup mold and chill well. Unmold on plate and serve with crackers. Can be made ahead and will keep for several days in the refrigerator. Makes about 3 cups.

Fish Cubes with Soy Dip

A sweet-sour dip with Mako shark will probably be a mystery fish combination to your guests.

1½ pounds Mako shark
2 tablespoons oil
2 tablespoons lime juice
½ cup orange marmalade
2 tablespoons lemon juice
2 tablespoons soy sauce
1 clove garlic, pressed
Freshly grated ginger to taste

Have Mako cut about 1 inch thick. Spread with oil and lime juice. Broil 3 to 4 inches from source of heat about 8 minutes, turning once. When cooled cut into ½-inch cubes. Mix remaining ingredients and serve in a bowl. Have picks available to dip mako in sweet-sour sauce as eaten.

· CLAMS ·

Hard-shell clams are all of the same family. Their name often indicates their size. Littlenecks, cherrystones, and quahogs (or chowder clams) are the ones found most commonly in the fish market. Littlenecks can be eaten raw or steamed, as can cherrystones.

Quahogs are large enough to be considered "tough" and are primarily chopped and used for chowder or fritters.

Soft-shelled clams are called steamers and are usually served that way.

Sea or surf clams are large clams, sometimes up to 8 inches long, that are harvested from the ocean waters. They are chopped and used for chowder or clam pie.

Directions for cleaning and opening hard-shelled clams are found in the chapter on Chowders and Soups.

Clams Casino

This popular classic is almost always made the same way. It make a fine appetizer or can be served as a first course.

24 cherrystone clams, cleaned
Finely chopped green pepper
Finely chopped red pepper*
Bacon slices cut to size of clams

Open clams and loosen from bottom of shell but do not remove. Discard one shell. Cover each clam with about ½ teaspoon each of chopped green and red pepper. Place bacon pieces on top of vegetables.

Place on broiler pan and broil, 4 inches from source of heat, 4 to 6 minutes or until bacon is crisp. This recipe can be enlarged depending on the number of people and their appetites. The clams can also be prepared in advance, refrigerated, and cooked when ready to eat.

*If red pepper is not available, use finely cut canned pimiento.

Hot Clam Fritters

An electric skillet where the temperature can be regulated is the best for cooking these tiny fritters. They always make a hit; if your party is in the family room, cook them in front of the guests.

½ cup all-purpose flour
1 teaspoon baking powder
1 egg, beaten
2 cups chopped raw clams, drained
1 teaspoon grated onion
Oil for frying

Mix flour and baking powder in a bowl. Add egg, clams, and onion and mix just until blended. Drop by teaspoons into 2 inches of oil heated to 375° F and fry until lightly browned, probably about 2 minutes. With a slotted spoon remove to paper toweling. The fritters can be kept hot in a 200° F oven. This recipe makes about 50 fritters. If you desire, serve with catsup or honey for dipping.

Roasted Clams

This simple way to serve clams as a first course or hors d'oeuvre is ideal for outdoor parties. The smell of the roasted clams is enticing.

Scrub and rinse well as many cherrystone or littleneck clams as you think will be eaten.

Put them on the grill over gray charcoal coals and let them stay there until they open. Have tongs handy to remove the clams to bowls or plates. Serve with lemon wedges. Forks (small cocktail forks, if available) are a necessity to loosen the clams from their shells.

Clam Dip

This clam dip is an old time favorite. It is better made the day before to let the flavors blend. Garnish with parsley and radishes.

> 1 cup chopped raw clams, drained
> 1 package (8 ounces) cream cheese, softened
> 1 tablespoon lemon juice
> 1 tablespoon grated onion
> 1 teaspoon chopped fresh parsley
> 1/8 teaspoon Tabasco sauce
> Assorted potato chips

Combine all ingredients except chips. Beat until well blended. If a creamier dip is desired add a little clam juice, if available, or light cream. Chill dip to let flavors blend. Serve with assorted potato chips. Makes about 1½ cups.

Stuffed Quahogs

Stuffed quahogs can be prepared in advance and frozen, ready to defrost and cook for a party. They are a perennial Cape favorite for entertaining because they are so popular with guests.

1 dozen quahogs
½ cup chopped onion
1 can (4 ounces) mushroom pieces, drained
¼ cup butter or margarine
3 tablespoons flour
Salt and freshly ground pepper to taste
½ cup buttered dry bread crumbs

Choose quahogs 3 to 4 inches in size, if possible. Clean and open quahogs (see instructions in Chowders and Soups). Wash shells.

Chop quahog meat. Cook onion and mushroom in butter until onion is tender. Blend in flour and salt and pepper. Add chopped clams and cook, stirring constantly, for 2 to 3 minutes. Butter clam shells and fill with mixture. Sprinkle crumbs over filling. Bake at 400° F for 10 minutes or until browned. Makes 1 dozen or more, depending on size of clams. Serve with forks.

* * *

Quick Hot Crabmeat Appetizer

Here is a quickly prepared hot appetizer using crabmeat. There is a mock crab product made of pollock and crab, which is considerably less expensive than regular crab. You might like to try it. I have and find it very good for the price.

1 cup cooked crabmeat
½ can condensed cream of mushroom soup
1 tablespoon finely chopped pimiento
1 tablespoon finely chopped green pepper
2½ to 3 dozen round crackers or bread rounds
Grated Parmesan cheese

Remove spines from crabmeat. Mix with mushroom soup and heat. Add pimiento and green pepper. Toast crackers or bread rounds on one side under the broiler. On untoasted side spread crabmeat mixture. Sprinkle with cheese. Heat under broiler until lightly browned. Makes about 2½ dozen.

· MUSSELS ·

Mussels have been around for a long time. In fact, the Indians introduced the Pilgrims to mussels, and mussels were probably a part of the first Thanksgiving menu. In Europe, where clams are not plentiful, mussels are a favorite. But here on the Cape clams were plentiful and easy to harvest and usurped the mussel in popularity. Until the last few years mussels were largely ignored by fishermen and fish markets. Recently, however, with private and government aid, consumers have been made more aware of the succulent mussel.

Mussels are a healthy food. They are an excellent source of potassium and a good source of phosphorus, iron, and magnesium as well as trace minerals. A 5.3-ounce portion of mussel meat has 117 calories. Also, the mussel is one of nature's most easily digestible foods.

Chill mussels from market to home in a cooler. Use within 2 days or cook and freeze the meat if they cannot be consumed during the 2-day period. It goes without saying that they should be refrigerated during storage.

If you purchase mussels that have been cultured in special areas of the ocean, there may not be much cleaning needed. Wild mussels, on the other hand, do require cleaning. They attach themselves to rocks, wooden piers, and in fact any place in the salt water where they can grow, even in eel grass. The fibrous growth that enables them to cling and grow in one place is called the beard and must be removed before cooking.

Mussels have shiny, blue-black shells. First discard any mussels that are open or feel heavy, as the shells probably are full of dirt. Then scrub shells lightly. Since the mussels do not burrow into the sand as clams do, scrubbing is not much of a problem. Use a small sharp knife to cut and pull the beard off. Rinse once more and the mussels are ready to cook. Two-inch-long mussels run about 20 to the pound.

Hot Mussel Hors D'Oeuvres

These garlicky mussels are good hot or cold as an accompaniment to most any beverage. Thinly sliced French bread may be served with the mussels, if desired.

>   2 pounds mussels
>   ¼ cup chopped onion
>   2 cloves garlic, finely chopped
>   2 tablespoons olive oil, butter, or margarine
>   ¼ cup dry white wine
>   Chopped fresh parsley

Clean mussels as directed. Put onions, garlic, olive oil, and white wine in a large saucepan. Add mussels, cover, bring to a boil, and cook over medium heat for about 4 minutes. Shake pan to allow mussels to cook evenly.

Remove mussels from pan, discarding any that do not open. Place in a dish. Sprinkle with chopped parsley. Strain broth into a bowl. With fingers, picks, or fish forks, dip mussels into broth and enjoy.

Cold Mussel Hors d'Oeuvres

The cooked mussels (preceding recipe) can be chilled and served cold. You can dip cold mussels in curried mayonnaise, below. Or remove one half of shell from cooked mussels, leaving mussel in other half. Spread mussel with curried mayonnaise and serve with picks or forks.

Curried Mayonnaise

>   1 cup mayonnaise
>   3 tablespoons fresh lemon juice
>   1 teaspoon grated onion
>   1 teaspoon curry powder (or more to taste)

Mix all ingredients. Serve chilled. About 1 cup.

Marinated Mussels

This is an appetizer that can be prepared in advance. Marinated mussels can also be used as a salad.

> 3 quarts mussels (about 3 pounds)
> ½ cup dry white wine
> 2 tablespoons chopped parsley

Marinade

> ½ cup olive oil
> 3 tablespoons lemon juice
> 2 cloves garlic, crushed
> 1 teaspoon chopped fresh tarragon leaves or ⅓ teaspoon dried
> Dash of Tabasco sauce
> Salt and freshly ground pepper to taste

Scrub mussels and remove beards. Rinse well. Put in a large pot with wine and parsley. Bring to a boil, cover, and cook until mussels open, about 4 to 5 minutes. Cool mussels. Discard any that do not open.

Remove mussels from shells and put into a glass jar. Mix olive oil with remaining ingredients and pour marinade over mussels. Cover and chill in refrigerator overnight or for 24 hours. Serve as an hors d'oeuvre with buttered party rye slices. Makes about 3 cups.

Marinated Mussels in Salad

Drain marinated mussels. Mix with ½ cup mayonnaise, ½ cup chopped celery, and 2 green onions, chopped. Serve in halves of ripe avocado and garnish with tomato wedges.

· OYSTERS ·

The traditional rule of thumb holds that oysters "R" in season, meaning that they should be eaten only during months with an R in their name. This tradition developed during times when summer icing was not as good as it is now; it also allowed a few spring and summer months for young oysters to grow to harvesting size. Today shucked oysters can be frozen and those in the shell are well iced at fish markets, so it is possible to buy them in the so-called off season. However, oysters will still be less plentiful and therefore more expensive out of season.

One way to shuck oysters: Scrub well with a stiff brush, rinse, and dry. Put oysters in the freezer for about 15 minutes. Remove from freezer and break off the thin end of the shells. Hold oyster in palm of hand with hinged end facing you. Force an oyster knife between the shells at the broken end, twisting to force the shells apart, and cut the large muscle close to the flat upper shell. Slide knife under oyster to release. An oyster knife has a short, stiff sharp blade.

Another way to open oysters is with a beer can opener. Put point of beer can opener at pointed end of oyster and raise to open shell.

Of course, you can always buy shucked oysters in the fish market by the pint, half pint, or what have you. As a rule, one pint contains in the neighborhood of 18 oysters. A lot of people I know collect enough shells to satisfy the number they need. Washed and dried after use and stored in a plastic bag, they are ready for the next appearance.

P.S. If you are a tyro at opening oysters, a heavy glove on the hand holding the oyster is a good idea.

Marinated Oysters

Marinated oysters have a nippy flavor that is wonderful. Serve ice cold.

1 pint oysters, fresh or frozen, defrosted
¼ cup tarragon vinegar
½ cup olive oil
1 clove garlic, crushed
Salt and freshly ground pepper to taste
½ teaspoon dried oregano leaves, crushed
Chopped fresh parsley
Cocktail rye bread slices, buttered

Drain oysters and remove any pieces of shell. Combine vinegar, oil, garlic, salt and pepper, and oregano. Add oysters and chill in refrigerator overnight or longer. When ready to serve, use a slotted spoon to remove oysters from marinade. Put them in a bowl, sprinkle with parsley, and serve on a plate surrounded by buttered cocktail rye bread slices. Makes about 18 servings.

Oysters and Mushrooms en Brochette

This oyster hor d'oeuvre can be prepared in advance, refrigerated, and broiled just before serving. The thin bamboo skewers are obtainable in specialty food stores and should be soaked in water 30 minutes before using.

1½ pints oysters
2 dozen small mushroom caps
8 to 12 slices bacon
24 small bamboo skewers, soaked 30 minutes (optional)

Drain oysters and remove any shell pieces.

Put one oyster and one mushroom cap on a part of a bacon slice (½ to ⅓ depending on size) and wrap bacon around oyster and mushroom. Secure with toothpick. Cook under broiler 3 to 4 inches from source of heat, turning, until bacon is crisp, about 3 to 5 minutes. Serve hot. Makes 24.

To use the wooden skewers, run the soaked skewer through bacon, oyster and mushroom just before broiling and remove toothpick.

Oyster Combo

Another oyster en brochette, this is a little more elaborate to prepare but a lovely mixing of flavors.

1 pint oysters
18 cherry tomatoes
18 cubes baby Swiss cheese*
½ cup (about) melted butter or margarine
Seasoned bread crumbs
18 small bamboo skewers, soaked 30 minutes

Drain oysters and pick out any pieces of shell. Dry on paper towels. Wash and dry tomatoes. Dip cheese, tomatoes, and oysters in melted butter, then roll in seasoned bread crumbs. Put one of each on each skewer. Broil 4 inches from source of heat 3 to 4 minutes. Serve hot. Makes 18.

*Baby Swiss cheese, available in deli sections of supermarkets, has Swiss cheese flavor but very small holes, so that it's easy to cube.

Hot Oysters

People are always impressed with oysters in the half shell. This combination of ingredients is a great foil for the oyster flavor.

1½ dozen oysters in the shell
1 clove garlic, pressed
¼ cup melted butter or margarine
¼ cup fresh lemon juice
1½ tablespoons white wine
1 teaspoon finely chopped chives

Wash and open oysters as directed. Leave oysters in deepest shell half. Discard other half shell. Refrigerate oysters until cooking time.

Mix remaining ingredients and let stand for about an hour. When ready to serve, place oysters on a broiler rack and divide sauce over them. Broil 3 to 4 inches from source of heat for 4 to 5 minutes or until oysters begin to curl at edges. Do not overcook. Serve hot.

* * *

Scallops Portuguese

When scallops are in season or you have gone scalloping, try this for a party.

1 pound bay or ocean scallops
¼ cup butter or margarine
1 clove garlic, minced
¼ teaspoon salt
Freshly ground pepper to taste
½ cup chopped fresh parsley

If ocean scallops are used, cut in half. (See information on scallops in Entrees.)

Pat dry with paper toweling. Melt butter or margarine. Add garlic and salt and cook until garlic is light brown. Add scallops and cook about 5 minutes, stirring. Sprinkle with pepper. Add chopped parsley and cook 1 minute longer. Serve hot in a chafing dish with picks.

· SHRIMP ·

Shrimp is one of the most popular appetizers you can serve. Fresh shrimp can be purchased "green," which means raw in the shell; cooked, still in the shell; or cooked and shelled. It also comes in different sizes. Tiny shrimp come about 60 to the pound. Medium shrimp are 25 to 30 to the pound, while jumbo shrimp are 15 or less to the pound. For appetizers, the tiny shrimp make up into excellent pates. The medium size are best for dipping into a sauce. The jumbo size should be reserved for baked stuffed shrimp.

Shrimp is also sold frozen as well as fresh.

If cooked shrimp is in the shell, remove shell and clean the sand vein by running a knife down the back curve of the shrimp and rinsing under cold water.

Raw shrimp in the shell will yield about half the purchased weight. In other words, 2 pounds of raw 30-per-pound count shrimp in the shell will yield about 1 pound after cooking and shelling.

Boiled Shrimp

Wash shrimp well. For 2 pounds medium shrimp in the shell (if frozen, defrost before cooking), put 6 cups water in a saucepan.* Add to the water ½ lemon, 1 medium bay leaf, 8 to 10 whole peppercorns, and salt to taste. Bring to a boil and cover. Boil for 15 minutes. Add shrimp and reduce heat. Simmer 3 to 5 minutes. Drain and rinse under cold water. Remove shells and sand vein and chill.

Serve with a dipping sauce made by mixing equal parts of chili sauce and catsup, seasoned to taste with Tabasco sauce, lemon juice, and horseradish.

*For an extra special flavor, beer can be substituted for water.

Broiled Shrimp

Remove shells and sand vein from 2 pounds medium shrimp. Mix together 3 cloves crushed garlic, ½ cup melted butter or margarine, 2 tablespoons fresh lime juice, and salt and freshly ground pepper to taste. Mix with shrimp, cover, and refrigerate for several hours. When ready to cook, remove garlic. Arrange shrimp in a single layer on broiler rack and broil 3 to 4 inches from source of heat for about 6 minutes. Serve hot.

Pink Shrimp Spread

This is an ideal party use for tiny shrimp. It is better when made ahead and chilled overnight.

> ½ pound cooked, peeled, deveined shrimp
> 1 can (10¾ ounces) condensed cream of mushroom soup
> 1 package (8 ounces) cream cheese, softened
> ¼ cup tomato paste
> 1 green onion, chopped
> Chopped fresh parsley
> Crackers or fresh vegetables

If the shrimp is frozen, defrost. Chop finely in the food processor with steel blade and remove to a bowl.

Add soup, cream cheese, tomato paste, and onion to food processor bowl and process with steel blade until completely blended. Add to shrimp and mix well. Spoon into a decorative bowl which holds 3 to 4 cups (or divide between two smaller bowls). Cover and chill. When ready to serve, circle outer edge of dip with chopped parsley. Serve with crackers or fresh vegetables. Makes 3½ cups.

· SQUID OR CALAMARI ·

Squid, or *calamari* in Italian, is a mollusk that is netted off the shores of the Cape. (A mollusk is a fish with a shell.) In the past a great deal of squid never even reached our shores; it was caught by foreign ships and either taken home to freeze or frozen right on board foreign factory ships. The squid came back to us from Portugal or Japan in 3- to 5-pound boxes, most of which were purchased for bait.

I remember the first time I bought squid. I found the 3-pound frozen box and asked the fish man if I could get less, since I only needed a pound for my recipe. He looked at me queerly and said, "Recipe, lady? Squid is only used for bait." I took the 3-pound box and discovered for the first time the many varied and good ways to cook squid.

Unfortunately, not too many fish markets carry squid because it is relatively pesky to clean and only true squid lovers are willing to clean their own. If the fish market cleans it the price goes up too high.

Here are directions as simple as I can make them.

If the squid are frozen, defrost completely in the refrigerator. Wash and dry. Cut off the tentacles just above the eyes with a sharp knife. Save.

Cut just below the eyes to remove the beak. Discard. Pull out the quill and entrails. Discard. Pull off purple skin and discard.

Rinse inside of squid. The squid is now ready to use as you wish. Do not cut body if you are to make stuffed squid. For a recipe such as vinaigrette cut as directed. Cut into rings for fried squid rings.

Calamari (Squid) Vinaigrette

A super appeteaser, as my neighbor used to say. Once the squid are cleaned the rest goes quickly.

> 3 pounds squid, cleaned
> 8 peppercorns
> 1 medium bay leaf
> 1 chili pepper
> 4 fresh parsley sprigs
> 1 clove garlic, crushed
> ¼ cup chopped fresh parsley
> ½ cup finely diced celery
> ¾ cup finely diced Spanish onion
> ¼ cup fresh lemon juice
> ¼ cup oil

Cut squid bodies into rings, tentacles into bite-size pieces. Put into a saucepan with cold water to cover. Add peppercorns, bay leaf, chili pepper, and parsley sprigs. Bring to a boil and let cook 1 minute. Cool squid in liquid. Drain, removing peppercorns, bay leaf, chili pepper, and parsley. Put into a bowl and add remaining ingredients, mixing lightly to blend. Mixture can be refrigerated, but to serve allow to come to room temperature. Serve with whole-wheat crackers.

Calamari (Squid) Appetizer

This pretty appetizer will probably surprise anyone who eats it without knowing it is squid. It is tasty and can be prepared in advance.

    2 pounds small fresh or frozen squid, cleaned
    1 clove garlic, minced
    ½ Spanish onion, chopped
    3 tablespoons oil
    ⅓ cup dry white wine
    1 jalapeno pepper, seeded and diced
    2 cups peeled plum tomatoes, diced
    Salt and freshly ground pepper to taste
    Chopped lettuce or romaine

Cut squid body into rings and dice tentacles. Combine garlic, onion, and oil in a saucepan and cook until onion is wilted. Add squid and saute for 3 minutes longer. Add wine, pepper, and tomatoes and cook 10 minutes. Chill. Season to taste with salt and pepper. Serve on chopped lettuce or romaine. Makes 4 to 6 servings as a first course.

Chowders
and
Soups

Seafood lends itself to chowder and soups from the simple to the so-
phisticated. Here on Cape Cod the only accepted version of New England clam chowder is made with salt pork (bacon can be substituted if
salt pork is not available), chopped clams, onions, potatoes, and milk.
Acceptable additions are soda or pilot crackers, butter, and a little
paprika or chopped parsley to color the top of the chowder after it is
served into bowls. With an influx of off-Cape visitors, a restaurant might
offer two versions, but it would never be without New England clam
chowder.

Other Cape recipes include fish chowder, made with any white-
fleshed fish; oyster stew; mussel soup; crab bisque; scallop stew; and
lobster stew or bisque. Then we branch out into our versions of Eu-
ropean recipes using both finfish and shellfish.

Whenever you get scraps of fish and bones, make fish stock (or fish
fumet, as the French call it). Freeze fish stock if it is not to be used at
once. It can help flavor soups and chowders and, indeed, other fish
dishes.

* * *

Anyone who lives on or near the Cape has access to fresh quahogs in
the shell or minced in containers. Lucky people get to go clamming
and dig their own.

Quahogs can be made into New England clam chowder, clam pie,
clam pancakes, clam fritters, or scalloped clams.

Clams dig down into the sand of the river or ocean shore where they
are dug, so they are generally sandy. They should be scrubbed and
rinsed thoroughly. Some persons swear by putting a handful of cornmeal
in the water and letting the clams stand in it for 30 minutes or so. The

29

claim is that the cornmeal draws out the sand. Personally, I have never found that it made much difference.

Anyway, once the clams are scrubbed and rinsed, put them in the freezer for about 30 minutes to get them good and cold. This relaxes the muscles. One method of shelling quahogs is this: Hold clam in hand with hinge toward the palm of the hand. (Wear a glove if you are new at this.) Grip clam firmly and insert blade of a clam knife between the top and bottom shells. Slide blade toward the hinge until the muscle is severed. The clam can then be freed from both halves of the shell. Save the juice as it can be used in cooking.

The way I do it is this: I put the clam upright on a board on the flat (hinge) edge. I insert the knife between the two curved top edges and then I pound the knife down with a wooden hammer (mallet) to open the clam. I quickly pick up the clam to drain the juice off into a bowl and cut out the clam into another bowl. This method I learned from our neighbor who has been a shellfish warden for years.

Before using quahogs, some prefer to remove the stomach, the yellow part in the middle of the clam. It is your own choice.

To give you an idea of the number of quahogs you need, 8 clams averaging 3 to 4 inches will yield about 1 cup chopped clams and 1¼ cups juice.

If you buy the chopped clams at a fish market, they will generally ask you if you want clam juice. It comes packaged separately.

New England Clam Chowder

If you want to start a discussion, the proper way to make New England clam chowder is a good place to begin. Here is one version.

2 dozen quahogs or 3 cups minced clams
¼ pound salt pork or bacon, minced
½ cup finely chopped onion
1½ cups clam juice (add water to make measure,
    if necessary)
5 cups diced raw potatoes
2 cups milk
8 single saltine crackers
2 cups half-and-half
2 tablespoons butter or margarine
Chopped parsley or paprika

Clean, and open, and chop clams. The easiest way to chop clams is in a food processor with the steel blade.

Fry the salt pork or bacon until browned. Remove from pan and reserve. Add onion to fat in pan and cook until tender, not browned. Add clam liquor (plus water if necessary to make 1½ cups) and potatoes. Bring to a boil and simmer until potatoes are tender, about 15 minutes. Pour milk over crackers and let stand until crackers are soft. Stir cracker and milk mixture, half-and-half, cooked salt pork, clams, and butter into potatoes. Heat until hot enough to serve. Do not boil. Garnish with chopped parsley or paprika. Makes 12 cups.

Clam Soup

A distinct variation from clam chowder and very good. Since I always have an excess of clam juice from clamming, this is one way to use it.

    2 cloves garlic, pressed
    4 tablespoons butter or margarine
    4 tablespoons flour
    1 cup chopped clams
    3 cups clam juice
    Squeeze of lime juice to taste
    Freshly ground pepper to taste

Saute garlic with butter and flour for 2 minutes. Add remaining ingredients and cook and stir until mixture boils and is thickened. Makes 4 cups.

New England Fish Chowder

When clams are expensive or hard to get, New England fish chowder is a fine substitute. Ask your fish market for "chowder fish." Very often small pieces of fish for chowder sell for less than regular fillets.

1 pound white-fleshed fish for chowder
1 slice bacon, diced, or 2 tablespoons chopped salt pork
½ cup chopped onion
1½ cups boiling water
2½ cups diced raw potatoes
2 cups milk
Salt and freshly ground pepper to taste
1 tablespoon butter or margarine
Chopped fresh parsley or paprika

Remove skin and bones from fish and cut into 1-inch cubes.

In a 2½-quart saucepan fry bacon or salt pork until crisp. Add onion and fry until tender but not browned. Add water and potatoes and simmer covered about 15 minutes until potatoes are tender.

Add milk, fish, and salt and pepper to taste. Cook below boiling point until milk is hot and fish flakes (do not boil). Stir in butter. Serve garnished with parsley or paprika. Makes about 7 cups.

Baked Chowder

Smoked haddock is also known as finnan haddie. For a hearty lunch or supper serve Baked Chowder with pilot crackers or large hunks of hot bread, a bowl of relishes, and fresh fruit in season.

1 pound smoked haddock (finnan haddie)
Cold water
¼ cup diced salt pork
1 cup chopped onion
2 cups diced raw potatoes
Salt and freshly ground pepper to taste
1 quart whole milk
2 tablespoons chopped parsley
Butter

Cover smoked haddock with cold water and soak for 1 hour. Cook salt pork until crisp. Add onion and continue cooking until onion is tender but not browned. Drain fish. Remove any bones. Place in buttered 2-quart baking dish. Spoon salt pork, onions, potatoes, and seasonings over fish. Heat milk to boiling and pour over food in casserole. Cover and bake at 375° F for 45 minutes or until potatoes are tender. Before serving, flake haddock. Serve in bowls. Makes 8 cups.

Jesse's Bluefish Chowder

When bluefish are abundant, make a hearty bluefish chowder. Serve it in cups for a first course to a meal or in bowls. Crackers, a plate of assorted sandwiches, and big glasses of cold skim milk would taste good with the bowls of chowder. Fresh fruit in season and cookies will round out the menu.

> 1 to 1½ pounds bluefish fillets
> 2 cups water
> ¼ cup finely chopped salt pork
> 1 medium onion, chopped
> 1 medium green pepper, seeded and chopped
> 3 medium potatoes, peeled and diced
> 1 can (10½ ounces) condensed cream of celery soup
> 1 can (13 ounces) evaporated milk or 1⅓ cups light
>   cream

Poach fillets in 2 cups water for 8 to 10 minutes. Cool enough to remove skin, dark flesh, and bones, if any. Save liquid for chowder.

Fry salt pork until crisp in a large saucepan. Remove and reserve. Add onion and green pepper to fat and cook until tender, not browned. Add fish liquid and potatoes. Simmer, covered, 10 minutes or until potatoes are tender. Add soup, evaporated milk, and fish, stirring to blend with potatoes. Cover and simmer just below the boiling point for 10 minutes. Stir occasionally. Serve with salt pork sprinkled on top of chowder. Makes about 1½ quarts.

Fish Muddle

This recipe for Fish Muddle — don't you love the title — comes from a government publication of a few years back. It is a thick soup and you will like it as much as I did.

1 pound haddock, cod, or other white fish (boneless)
1 pound pork sausage meat
1½ cups fresh bread crumbs
1 cup minced onion
1 egg, beaten
1 teaspoon dried marjoram leaves, crushed
¼ teaspoon leaf thyme, crushed
Freshly ground pepper to taste
1 tablespoon oil
1 cup water
½ teaspoon salt
6 cups half-and-half
½ cup instant mashed potato
¼ cup chopped parsley
2 chopped hard-cooked eggs

Cut fish into 6 portions.

Combine sausage, bread crumbs, ½ cup of the minced onion, egg, and seasonings, mixing well. Shape into balls using about 1 tablespoon mixture per ball. In a 5-quart Dutch oven heat oil and add meat balls and brown. Add remaining onion and cook until onion is tender. Add water and simmer, covered, 10 to 15 minutes. Place fish fillets on top of meat balls. Add salt and pour half-and-half over fish. Heat until fish flakes easily, 3 to 4 minutes after half-and-half is hot. Stir in instant potatoes until mixture is thick. Stir in parsley. To serve, ladle into soup bowls and sprinkle with chopped eggs. Makes about 12 cups.

Northwest Fish Chowder

Just in case someday you should like a change of pace in fish chowder, we've borrowed this recipe from Alaska. Serve it with pilot crackers or big chunks of hot Italian bread.

> 1 cup chopped onion
> 1 cup chopped zucchini
> ¼ cup oil
> 1 can (1 pound) tomatoes
> 2 cups tomato juice
> ⅓ cup white wine or water
> ¾ teaspoon salt
> 1½ tablespoons chopped fresh basil or 1½ teaspoons
>   dried, crushed basil
> Dash Tabasco sauce
> 1½ pounds boneless cod, tautog, or hake fillets

Cook onion and zucchini in oil in a good sized heavy saucepan until soft, not browned. Add tomatoes, juice, wine, and seasonings. Cover and simmer 10 to 15 minutes. Cut fish into bite-size pieces and add to tomatoes. Simmer about 5 minutes or until fish flakes. Can be refrigerated and reheated. Will keep about 3 days under refrigeration. Makes 7 cups.

Tautog Chowder

This Tautog Chowder can be made from the entire fish, from fresh or frozen fillets, or by boiling the frames after filleting. (Save the meat and stock and discard any skin and bones.) For each pound of meat, use at least two cups of water. For lunch or supper, a salad and crackers or bread make a meal.

1 pound tautog, fresh or frozen
2 tablespoons chopped bacon or salt pork
½ medium onion, chopped
2½ medium potatoes, peeled and diced
2 cups water
2 stalks celery, diced
½ teaspoon salt
Freshly ground pepper to taste
Snipped fresh dill to taste (if desired)
2 cups milk
1 tablespoon butter or margarine
Chopped parsley (if desired)

If you have made a chowder base by boiling the fish, remove skin and any bones. Strain liquid.

Fry bacon until crisp. Add onion and cook until tender. Add to fish broth along with potatoes, celery, seasonings. (If starting from fillets, add fish and 2 cups water to bacon and onion, potatoes, and seasonings.) Cover and simmer about 20 minutes until potatoes are tender. Add milk and butter; heat, but do not boil. Sprinkle parsley on chowder. Makes 6 cups.

Oyster Stew

Oyster stew is another of those recipes that has devotees of different basic ingredients. This is a Cape Cod version — and you can add your own variations.

> 1 pint raw oysters (if frozen, defrost)
> ¼ cup butter or margarine
> 2 cups milk, scalded*
> 2 cups light cream, scalded*
> Salt to taste
> Paprika

Pick out pieces of shell that might be in the oysters. Heat butter in a skillet, add oysters and their liquid, and cook and stir until edges of oysters start to curl. This takes just a few minutes. Add to hot milk and cream and add salt to taste. Serve at once or hold below boiling point 10 minutes to blend flavors. Add a dash of paprika to each serving. Makes 6 cups.

*4 cups half-and-half can be substituted for the milk and cream.

Mussel Soup

Lots of crusty bread and a tossed green salad go well with this hearty soup.

5 dozen mussels
1 or 2 bay leaves
1 onion, chopped
1 quart water
1 leek, white part only
2 tablespoons olive oil
½ cup rice
Salt and freshly ground pepper to taste

Scrub and debeard mussels (see instructions in Appetizers). Rinse and put into a large saucepan with bay leaves, chopped onion, and water. Cover and cook 3 to 5 minutes until the shells open. Discard any that do not open. Pour liquid through a sieve into a bowl. Remove mussels from shells and set aside.

Clean leek well to remove sand, then chop. Heat oil in a large saucepan and cook leek until lightly browned. Add liquid from mussels, rice, and salt and pepper to taste. Simmer 15 to 20 minutes or until rice is tender. Add mussels and simmer just long enough to heat. Serve in bowls. Makes 8 cups.

Variation: Add chopped fresh tomato to mussel liquid when cooking rice.

Crab Bisque

This easily made and elegant soup is equally good hot or chilled. Garnish with croutons, whipped cream, or chopped parsley.

1 can (10¾ ounces) condensed cream of mushroom soup
1 can (10½ ounces) condensed cream of asparagus soup
1 cup crabmeat, spines removed
2 cups half-and-half
½ cup dry sherry
1 teaspoon Angostura bitters

Combine soups and crabmeat (in 2 batches) in food processor with steel blade or blender. Process until smooth. Put in saucepan and add remaining ingredients. Stir to blend. Heat to boiling point, but do not boil. Makes 8 cups. May be served hot or chilled.

Scallop Stew

When scallops are in season — fall and winter — this is a good way to stretch their distinctive flavor.

1 pound scallops, bay or ocean
4 tablespoons butter or margarine
¼ cup chopped onion
1 potato, peeled and finely diced
Water
1 quart milk
Salt and freshly ground pepper to taste
Chopped fresh parsley

Wash and remove any pieces of shell from scallops. Cut large scallops into ½-inch pieces. Heat butter in a 2-quart saucepan. Saute onion and potato until onion is tender but not browned. Cover with water. Cover pan and simmer 10 minutes or until potatoes are tender enough to mash with a fork; mash. Add milk and bring to simmering point. Do not boil. Stir in scallops and heat below boiling for 5 minutes. To serve, sprinkle with parsley. Makes 6 cups.

Lobster Stew

Lobster Stew, like lobster salad, should be pure and simple. It's lobster, tomalley, coral (if available), butter, and rich milk. Nothing else!

1 lobster (2 pounds), cooked
Tomalley
Coral, if available
½ cup butter
1 pint whole milk
1 pint half-and-half

Remove meat from lobster shell and cut into medium size pieces.
Saute tomally and coral in butter, stirring to blend, for about 10 minutes. Add lobster and cook just long enough to heat through. Remove from heat and very slowly add milk, stirring constantly, then half-and-half, continuing to stir. Refrigerate stew 5 to 6 hours before reheating to serve. Do not boil. Makes 6 cups.

Lobster Bisque

When you go into a fish market and see the red body parts of the lobster you may wonder what they are good for besides decorating the fish counter. They are inexpensive (as a rule) and can be used for a delicious Lobster Bisque.

3 or 4 lobster bodies
½ cup celery leaves
1 small onion
8 peppercorns
7 cups water (about)
½ cup diced carrots
½ cup diced celery
½ cup chopped onion
4 tablespoons butter or margarine
4 tablespoons flour
¼ cup dry white wine

There is lobster meat in the bodies. Take a nut pick, get out as much as you can, and refrigerate it. Crush the lobster bodies and put them in a saucepan with celery leaves, small whole onion, peppercorns and enough water to cover lobster shells. Bring to a boil. Cover and simmer slowly about 1 hour. Cool a little, strain, and discard solids. Boil to reduce liquid to 3 cups.

Meanwhile saute carrots, celery, and chopped onions in butter until just tender. Stir in flour, reduced liquid, and wine. Cook and stir until mixture boils and is thickened. Add any lobster meat you garnered and cook long enough to heat. Serve with a dollop of whipped cream, if desired. Makes 4 cups.

Fish Bisque

A simple recipe which brings out the flavor of the fish.

2 pounds boneless pollock fillets
Cold water to cover
1 small onion, finely chopped
¼ cup butter or margarine
¼ cup flour
2 cups half-and-half
Salt and freshly ground pepper to taste
1 tablespoon chopped fresh parsley

Cut fillets into small pieces. Place in a skillet and cover with cold water. Bring to a boil and simmer just below boiling point until fish flakes easily with a fork, 5 to 7 minutes. Cool a while to let flavor develop, then drain liquid and reserve.

Cook onion in butter until tender but not browned. Add flour and cook 2 minutes. Stir in half-and-half and cook and stir until mixture comes to a boil and is thickened. Add 2 cups liquid from fish and cook until heated through. Season to taste with salt and pepper. Add fish and hold below boiling point for 5 minutes. Serve in soup plates garnished with chopped parsley. Makes 8 cups.

Seafood Chowder

An elegant meal in itself is Seafood Chowder. Serve pilot crackers or crispy bread with this chowder.

2 dozen mussels
1 cup finely chopped celery
1 cup water
½ cup dry white wine
2 tablespoons lemon juice
½ pound green shrimp
½ cup butter
½ pound cooked lobster meat
3 cups mussel stock
1½ quarts half-and-half
2 tablespoons Worcestershire sauce

Combine cleaned mussels with celery, water, wine, and lemon juice in a large pan. Bring to a boil, cover, and let simmer 4 to 5 minutes or until mussels open. Discard any that do not open. Cool and remove mussels from shells. Discard shells. Measure liquid (including celery) and add water to make 3 cups, if necessary.

Peel and devein shrimp and saute in butter for 3 to 4 minutes or until pink. Cut lobster into medium pieces.

Mix mussel stock with half-and-half, Worcestershire sauce, shrimp and butter in which they were cooked, lobster, and mussels. Heat to boiling point. Serve with pilot crackers. Makes 11 cups.

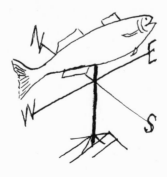

Seafood Medley

Seafood recipes of this kind probably originated in Spain or Portugal. This American version is a delicious way to use some of our Cape Cod sea treasures.

1 small onion, chopped
2 tablespoons olive oil
1 teaspoon Dijon type mustard
2 cups clam broth
2 cups peeled and chopped ripe tomatoes
1 carrot, finely chopped
1 stalk celery, finely chopped
½ teaspoon salt
½ teaspoon paprika
¼ teaspoon dried oregano
1 clove garlic, finely chopped
1 bay leaf
½ pound green shrimp, shelled and deveined
½ pound bay or ocean scallops
½ pint oysters
½ pound crabmeat
1 pound fillet of sole or flounder
Melted butter

In a large Dutch oven saute onion in olive oil until tender, not browned. Add mustard, clam broth, vegetables, and seasonings. Cover and simmer 1 hour, stirring now and then. Remove bay leaf. Add shrimp and scallops and cook 5 minutes longer. Stir in oysters and crabmeat.

Meanwhile, cut fish fillets into 6 portions. Spread with melted butter and broil 4 inches from heat 6 to 8 minutes.

To serve, put a piece of fish in bottom of each bowl and ladle on fish and vegetable mixture. Makes 12 cups.

Portuguese Fish Stew

This Portuguese recipe is similar to a traditional South American stew recipe except that it is made with fish instead of meat. It is what I call a soup-stew.

2 pounds black bass fillets or other fish fillets
1 tablespoon butter or margarine
1 cup chopped Spanish onion
1 clove garlic, crushed
2 cans (1 pound each) tomatoes
3 cups water
1 teaspoon each dried basil and thyme, crushed
¼ teaspoon dried red pepper, crushed
1 teaspoon salt
4 cups fresh pumpkin or winter squash, peeled and cut in 1-inch cubes
2 ears corn, cut crosswise into 2-inch pieces

Cut fish into 1-inch pieces and remove bones, if any.

In a large saucepan melt butter and add onion and garlic. Cook until onion is tender. Cut tomatoes into pieces and add with their juice, water, seasonings, pumpkin, and corn to onions. Bring to a boil and simmer, covered, 15 minutes or until pumpkin is tender. Add fish and cook 5 to 8 minutes longer or until it flakes easily with a fork.

Serve in bowls with toasted Portuguese or French bread. Makes 12 cups.

Fish Stock or Fish Fumet

If a certain fish dealer remembers me, he probably thinks I'm the biggest nut he has run into. I had read a recipe that used fish heads — I think it came from Hong Kong — and I decided it would be fun to try it. So one of my friends directed me to a place where fish was prepared for wholesale outlets and I could get all the fish heads I wanted. They weren't exactly small and I mean I could have gotten all I wanted, up to a truckload or two. I finally made the man understand that three was enough and carted them home to prepare the recipe. It never crossed my mind what the eyes would look like after the fish heads had been cooked. They really stared at me, and I had a difficult time finishing the dish. P.S. It wasn't all that good.

All this preamble is to point out that many recipes call for fish stock, and stock is often made from fish heads. This is a simple recipe. Ask at the fish market if they have fish bones or heads to use for stock. Ignore the eyes.

Bones from a good sized fish*
1 medium onion
1 carrot, sliced
1 stalk celery, sliced
1 sprig parsley
8 peppercorns
Salt to taste
1 small bay leaf
¼ teaspoon dried thyme leaves
1 cup dry white wine
1½ cups water

In a large saucepan combine all ingredients. Bring to a boil and simmer, covered, about 30 minutes. Cool. Strain. If the fish bones had any appreciable amount of flesh on them, remove bones with a slotted spoon and use fish flesh for salad.

Fish stock may be used at once, or it may be frozen for future use. If possible, freeze stock in 1-cup containers, as this amount is usable in most recipes. This recipe makes about 3 cups. If you use a great deal of fish stock, the recipe can be multiplied with no problems.

*Scrap pieces of fish may be used if fish bones are not available.

Salads
and
Cold Dishes

Probably the first fish salad most of us think of is tuna fish, generally meaning canned tuna. Next come lobster and shrimp, both wonderful though expensive. But practically any fish can be made into a salad. Poach or broil the fish until it flakes, remove bones and skin, then flake and chill. Treat it as a base for your favorite fish salad. Add a bit of lemon juice, chopped celery, hard-cooked eggs, a touch of chili sauce or catsup, mayonnaise, or other favorite dressing and you have a high-protein salad for lunch or dinner.

Or if you have leftover fish, add it to a salad of tossed greens or a macaroni salad. Cold cooked fish takes on and gives a new taste.

Serve fish salad in halves of avocado; or cut down tomatoes so that the sections can be spread like petals and pile the fish salad in the center.

If you want more color, decorate fish salad with green pepper strips, grated egg yolk, sliced pimiento-stuffed olives, slices of gherkins, radish roses, or anything colorful and edible that is in your larder.

* * *

47

Salmon and Walnut Salad

From my childhood I remember Salmon and Walnut Salad. It was always served with tomatoes from the garden and Mother's homemade bread. What a treat.

> 1 piece salmon, about 1 pound
> 1 cup fish stock (see recipe in Chowders and Soups)
> ½ cup dry white wine
> 1 small onion
> ½ lemon
> 2 sprigs parsley
> ½ cup coarsely chopped walnuts
> ½ cup finely chopped celery
> Salt and freshly ground pepper to taste
> ½ cup (about) mayonnaise
> Garden tomatoes
> Lettuce
> 2 hard-cooked eggs

Poach salmon in a stock made of the fish stock, wine, onion, lemon, and parsley until it flakes easily, about 8 to 10 minutes. Cool in liquid.

When cool, remove skin and bones and flake salmon into a bowl. Add walnuts, celery, salt and pepper, and mayonnaise, stirring lightly to blend ingredients. Chill well.

When ready to serve, slice tomatoes thinly. Arrange beds of lettuce on 4 plates, divide salmon salad among plates, and garnish with tomato slices and sliced hard-cooked eggs. Makes 4 servings.

Tuna Fish Salad

Occasionally one can find fresh tuna at the market. Poach it to make a truly beautiful salad.

1 pound fresh tuna
1 cup fish stock (see recipe in Chowders and Soups)
½ cup dry white wine
½ cup finely chopped celery
Salt and freshly ground pepper to taste
¼ cup sliced stuffed olives
½ cup mayonnaise
Crisp lettuce

Poach tuna in fish stock and dry white wine combined, below boiling point, for about 8 minutes or until fish flakes easily. Cool in liquid. Remove from liquid and take off skin and bones. Flake and chill. Add remaining ingredients except lettuce and chill again. Serve on crisp lettuce. Makes 4 servings. This dish is especially tasty if you use home-made mayonnaise, below.

Homemade Blender Mayonnaise

1 cup salad oil
2 tablespoons lemon juice
1½ teaspoons spicy prepared mustard
¼ teaspoon salt
1 egg

Combine ¼ cup salad oil, lemon juice, mustard, salt, and egg in blender. Run 15 seconds. Gradually add remaining oil. Stop blender and push mayonnaise down with a rubber spatula, if necessary, to blend in all of oil. Put mayonnaise into a jar, cover, and store in refrigerator. Makes 1½ cups.

Macaroni Fish Salad

For a luncheon menu, serve hot tomato bouillon as a first course. With the Macaroni Fish Salad, deviled eggs and corn muffins round out the main course. Fresh fruit will do nicely for dessert.

> 1 cup cooked small macaroni shells
> 2 cups cooked, flaked white fish
> 2 tablespoons lemon juice
> ½ cup chopped celery
> ¼ cup chopped green pepper
> ¼ cup drained pickle relish
> ½ cup mayonnaise
> 2 teaspoons Dijon style mustard
> Crisp lettuce

Combine macaroni with fish, lemon juice, celery, green pepper, and pickle relish and toss lightly. Mix mayonnaise and mustard and add to macaroni-fish mixture. Chill well. Serve on crisp lettuce. Makes 4 servings.

Lobster Salad

Some of my Cape friends were aghast when I suggested putting a little chopped celery in lobster salad. A true Cape Codder considers that lobster salad should be only lobster and mayonnaise with perhaps a wedge of lemon on the side. It's okay to serve it on lettuce, but very little.

> 3 cups cooked lobster meat
> 3 tablespoons mayonnaise
> Lettuce
> Lemon wedges (optional)

Chill the lobster and cut it into small pieces. Mix lightly with the mayonnaise — use mayonnaise, not salad dressing. Chill again. (If you find you need a little more mayonnaise, go ahead and add it.) Serve on crisp lettuce. Makes 4 servings.

Lobster Rolls

Another favorite way to serve lobster salad is called a lobster roll. The lobster salad is piled on toasted and buttered split frankfurter buns. And believe me it doesn't take long for the word to get around where the good lobster rolls are.

Not so incidentally, shrimp salad can be served the same way and it is good, too.

Mock Lobster Salad

Monkfish has a rather coarse texture and is ideal for a fish salad. With red pimiento added it becomes mock lobster!

2 pounds monkfish
1 cup fish stock (see recipe in Chowders and Soups)
1 cup dry white wine
1 sliced small onion
3 tablespoons pimiento cut in thin strips
3 tablespoons lemon juice
½ to ¾ cup mayonnaise
Salt to taste
Lettuce

Combine monkfish with fish stock, wine, and onion. Bring to a boil and simmer 8 to 10 minutes or until fish flakes. Remove from liquid and take off skin and bones. Cut fish in 1-inch chunks and chill well. Add all remaining ingredients except lettuce and toss lightly. Chill again. Serve on crisp lettuce. Makes 4 servings.

Mock Lobster Rolls

As with real lobster salad, you can serve this salad on toasted, buttered frankfurter rolls. The above amount will make about 6 rolls. Serve potato chips with the salad rolls.

Cape Cod Chef's Salad

What a dream salad. Serve with toasted French or Italian bread.

Chopped lettuce
1 cup cooked lobster meat
½ pound poached codfish, chilled
½ pound shrimp, cooked, peeled, and deveined
4 hard-cooked eggs
2 ripe tomatoes, cut in wedges
½ cup mayonnaise
¼ cup lime juice

In 4 individual salad bowls arrange a bed of chopped lettuce. Cut lobster into fairly small dice. Place a row of lobster down one side on lettuce in each bowl. Flake cod and make a row next to lobster, and on the other side of the cod make a row of shrimp cut into medium pieces. Decorate with hard-cooked eggs and tomato wedges. Combine mayonnaise and lime juice and serve with salad. Makes 4 servings.

Scallop Salad

Although scallops are more often served sauted or broiled, they can also be poached and used in a delicious salad. For a hot summer day serve jellied bouillon as a first course. Garnish the salad platter with garden ripe tomatoes and serve sandwiches of thin-sliced whole-wheat bread and butter. A simple dessert such as blueberries with ice cream would make the menu complete.

2 pounds bay or ocean scallops
1 cup mayonnaise
½ cup dairy sour cream
3 tablespoons minced onion
1 tablespoon prepared horseradish
Dash Tabasco sauce
2 teaspoons Dijon style mustard
¼ cup chopped stuffed olives
Crisp lettuce

Cut large ocean scallops in halves or quarters, or leave bay scallops whole. Poach in water just below the boiling point for about 5 minutes. Drain and chill. Combine with remaining ingredients except lettuce, mixing lightly to blend. Serve on crisp lettuce. Makes 6 servings.

Shrimp Salad

To make a lovely salad plate, serve shrimp salad and potato salad on crisp lettuce. Garnish the plate with gherkins and radishes. Serve hot buttered French bread with the salad. For dessert have orange or lemon sherbet and crisp cookies. Iced tea would make a good beverage.

> 1 pound medium shrimp
> ½ cup finely chopped celery
> ½ cup mayonnaise
> ½ cup heavy cream, whipped
> 2 tablespoons chopped fresh dill
> 2 tablespoons fresh lemon juice
> Salt and freshly ground pepper to taste
> Crisp lettuce
> 4 cherry tomatoes

Cook shrimp in boiling water for 2 minutes. Drain and chill in cold water. Shell, devein, and chop shrimp into medium pieces. Mix lightly with celery, mayonnaise, cream, dill, lemon juice, and salt and pepper to taste.

Serve in crisp lettuce cups and garnish with cherry tomatoes cut in petals. Makes 4 servings.

Shrimp and Bean Sprout Salad

A different combination with shrimp. The bean sprouts and water chestnuts add their crunchiness to the salad.

>1 pound bean sprouts*
>1 cup thinly sliced celery
>1 green onion, finely chopped
>1 cup sliced water chestnuts
>½ pound shrimp, cooked, peeled and deveined, and
>   diced
>2 tablespoons soy sauce
>2 tablespoons lime juice
>¼ cup mayonnaise
>Lettuce

Wash and dry bean sprouts. Combine with celery, onion, water chestnuts, and shrimp. Mix soy sauce, lime juice, and mayonnaise and toss lightly with bean sprout mixture. Serve on lettuce. Makes 4 servings.

*You can buy bean sprouts in many supermarkets, or grow your own. To grow your own, put ⅓ cup mung beans in a quart canning jar with a ring lid. Cover beans with water and let soak overnight. In the morning, rinse beans with fresh water and drain. Put a thin cloth over top of jar and hold in place with ring lid. Keep beans wet by watering and draining each day. Shake so that beans will not compact in the bottom of the jar. It takes about 3 days for all beans to sprout. Store in refrigerator, rinsing and draining as used. Will keep about 4 days. Use both beans and sprouts. Makes about 4 cups.

Cold Poached Bass

This is one of the best cold fish recipes I have ever tasted and worth all the work. It is a buffet dish which has brought raves when I've served it.

1 black or striped bass, tilefish, or cod, 4 to 5 pounds
4 cups water
1 small onion, sliced
3 sprigs parsley
1 teaspoon salt
6 peppercorns
1 cup dry white wine
1 recipe tomato rice stuffing (below)
1 recipe herbed mayonnaise (below)
Radish roses, cucumber slices, lemon slices

Clean bass and cut off head. Combine head with water, bring to boil, and simmer about 10 minutes. Strain liquid into a pan with seasonings and wine. (Discard head.) Cover liquid and simmer 15 minutes. Pour into a fish poacher or flat roasting pan large enough to hold bass. Wrap bass in clean cheesecloth and place in pan. Cover with wax paper. Bring liquid to a boil, reduce heat, and simmer 10 minutes. Turn fish and simmer 5 minutes longer. Cool fish in poaching liquid until it is possible to handle, but not cold. Hold fish by cheesecloth to remove from pan onto a large piece of foil. Starting at tail end, carefully remove skin from both sides. Slit fish down the back and cut down the front as necessary. Separate the halves of the fish and leave, skinned side down, on foil. Remove all bones. (If fish breaks don't worry as it can be pieced together when assembled later.) Wrap the fish carefully in the foil and chill in the refrigerator until ready to assemble.

To assemble, put one half of cooked bass on a long fish platter (or any platter long enough to hold fish nicely). Spread rice stuffing on fish. Put other half of fish on top of the stuffing. Spread fish with herbed mayonnaise. Garnish with radish roses, cucumber slices, and lemon slices. Serves about 8.

The finished fish can be stored in the refrigerator up to 2 hours.

Tomato Rice Stuffing

Cook ⅓ cup regular (not instant) rice in 1 cup water about 12 minutes. Drain and cool. Mix with ½ cup chopped peeled tomato, 1 teaspoon grated onion, ⅛ teaspoon dried dill weed, ½ teaspoon salt, and 1 tablespoon mayonnaise. Chill.

Herbed Mayonnaise

To ½ cup mayonnaise add 1 tablespoon chopped chives and 1 tablespoon chopped fresh parsley.

Cold Salmon or Swordfish en Gelee

This cold fish dish is a tasty beauty for a buffet or summer event.

1 piece (3 to 5 pounds) salmon or swordfish
1 quart water
½ lime, sliced
½ onion, sliced
3 sprigs parsley
6 peppercorns
1 teaspoon salt
1 bay leaf
1 envelope unflavored gelatin
Thinly sliced stuffed olives
Thinly sliced radishes
Thin green pepper slices
Thin lemon slices cut in halves or quarters
Parsley

SALADS AND COLD DISHES

Combine water, lime, onion, 3 sprigs parsley, and seasonings in a large shallow pan. Bring to a boil. Wrap fish in cheesecloth and immerse in boiling liquid. If necessary, add additional boiling water to cover fish. Cover, reduce heat, and simmer gently until fish flakes easily when tested with a fork at thickest part. Allow 10 minutes cooking time per inch of thickness measured at its thickest part. Remove fish from liquid with cheesecloth. Open cloth and cool fish enough to handle. Remove skin. Carefully put fish on a serving platter, discarding cheesecloth. Chill fish. Strain poaching liquid.

Soften gelatin in 2 cups cooled poaching liquid and heat to dissolve completely. Chill until mixture starts to thicken, then spoon a thin coating of mixture over fish, covering fish completely. Chill.

Garnish with olive slices radish slices, and green pepper and lemon slices to make flowers or abstract designs, placing carefully on fish. Just as carefully apply a second coat of the partially thickened gelatin so as not to disturb the pattern. Gelatin can be kept at room temperature and quickly chilled to proper thickness by setting pan in an ice bath. Let the fish chill, apply a third coat of gelatin, and chill again to set. Garnish the fish with parsley and it is ready to serve.

If desired, serve the fish with mayonnaise.

On a buffet table with other foods, the fish will probably serve 10 or 12. If served alone as an entree, plan for 6 servings.

Fish Mousse

Not a dish that you would whip up on your lunch hour, Fish Mousse is a spectacular for a special occasion.

1 pound white-fleshed fish (cod, haddock, ocean catfish)
1 bay leaf
Slice lemon
Parsley sprig
½ teaspoon dried tarragon
2 cups water
1½ packages unflavored gelatin
½ cup water
1 package (8 ounces) cream cheese, softened
⅓ cup catsup
1 cup mayonnaise
¾ cup finely chopped celery
2 green onions, finely chopped
2 tablespoons lemon juice
½ teaspoon steak sauce
Salt and freshly ground pepper to taste

Combine fish with bay leaf, lemon, parsley, tarragon, and 2 cups water in a skillet. Simmer 5 minutes or until fish flakes easily with a fork. Let cool in water.

Soften gelatin in ½ cup water. In a saucepan combine cheese with catsup and cook and stir over moderate heat until smooth and blended. Stir in softened gelatin and hold over heat until gelatin is dissolved. Let cool.

Drain fish, flake, and remove any bones and skin. Stir into cooled gelatin mixture with mayonnaise, celery, onion, lemon juice, and steak sauce. Taste and add salt and pepper if needed. Spoon into a 1-quart mold which has been rinsed with water and chill 2 hours or overnight. Cover loosely with wax paper or plastic wrap, Unmold to serve. Garnish as desired. Makes 6 servings.

Entrees

Seafood can be prepared in so many ways as the main dish of the meal that it is almost impossible to exhaust all the possibilities. Seafood dishes combine with a wide variety of pasta products and vegetables. If one prefers fish cooked in a plain style it is especially easy to plan menus around it, since almost any food fits.

This section is a sampling of the dozens of ways to prepare seafood and add variety to your diet in a healthful manner.

· FISH ·

Plain Broiled Bluefish

Blues, as many people call bluefish, are caught in the Atlantic and as far south as the Gulf. They are plentiful in Cape waters in the summer. These spririted game fish are a great catch for the nonprofessional fisherman. They generally weigh 3 to 6 pounds but can go up to 10. Bluefish have tasty flesh and can be cooked in many ways. Do not eat the skin or the black strips in the fish. Clean and split the bluefish. Place on a well-greased broiler pan and cover generously with lemon juice. Dot with butter and sprinkle with salt and pepper to taste. Broil 4 inches from source of heat for about 10 minutes or until fish flakes easily with a fork. Number of servings depends on size of bluefish.

Broiled Bluefish with Tomatoes

Broiled Bluefish with Tomatoes is an interesting way in which to serve bluefish. To go with the fish we get back to an old standby, potato salad along with sliced cucumbers and lettuce and rye bread. For dessert serve cantaloupe.

> 2 pounds bluefish fillets
> ¼ cup lemon juice
> Salt and freshly ground pepper to taste
> 1 small onion, peeled
> 1 ripe tomato
> 2 tablespoons chilled butter or margarine
> 6 sprigs parsley
> ¼ teaspoon dried tarragon leaves
> 1 slice whole-wheat bread, broken into pieces

Place bluefish fillets skin side down on an oiled broiler pan. Pour lemon juice over fillets and sprinkle with salt and pepper to taste. Put remaining ingredients in a blender or in a food processor with steel blade and blend. Broil fish 4 inches from source of heat for 5 minutes. Spread tomato mixture on fish and broil 3 to 5 minutes longer. Makes 4 servings.

Broiled Bluefish Fillets with Vermouth

With these bluefish fillets serve parslied new potatoes, Harvard beets, and a Waldorf salad to take care of both salad and dessert.

2 pounds bluefish fillets
2 tablespoons butter or margarine, softened
1 teaspoon fresh thyme leaves or ⅓ teaspoon dried
Salt and freshly ground pepper to taste
¼ cup dry vermouth
¼ cup water
1 tablespoon butter or margarine

Place fillets on oiled broiler pan skin side down. Spread with softened butter and sprinkle with thyme, salt, and pepper. Mix vermouth with water and spoon over fillets. Broil 2 to 3 inches from heat 6 to 8 minutes or until fish flakes easily with fork. Swirl remaining butter into pan juices and serve with fish. Makes 4 servings.

Baked Bluefish

This simple recipe for baked bluefish would go well with steamed potatoes, a vegetable in season such as zucchini or spinach, lettuce salad with cucumber dressing, and an easy dessert — perhaps pound cake with ice cream and fruit sauce.

1 bluefish, about 3 pounds
⅓ to ½ cup lemon juice
Butter or margarine
Salt and freshly ground pepper to taste
Lemon slices
Chopped parsley

Clean and split the bluefish. Place skin side down in a shallow pan and pour lemon juice over it. Let stand in refrigerator for at least an hour. Transfer to an oiled baking pan, skin side down, and dot fish with butter. Season to taste with salt and pepper. Bake at 425° F for 20 minutes, basting with lemon juice and butter. Test with fork to see if fish flakes readily. Serve with lemon slices and garnish with chopped parsley. Makes 4 servings.

Tropical Bluefish

It seems to me that no one is neutral about bluefish. You either like it or you don't. This recipe using tropical fruit juices should make a few more converts. Hot cooked rice, a green vegetable in season, three-bean salad, and toasted Italian bread can round out the main course.

> 1 cup minced onions
> 3 pounds bluefish fillets
> ¾ cup fresh orange juice
> 2 tablespoons fresh lemon juice
> ½ teaspoon salt
> Freshly ground pepper to taste
> 2 tablespoons chopped fresh parsley
> 2 limes cut in wedges

Sprinkle half of onion in a buttered flat baking dish. Arrange bluefish fillets on onion. Combine orange and lemon juice, salt, and pepper and pour over fish. Sprinkle remaining onions on top. Cover lightly and let stand in refrigerator for about 1 hour.

Bake fish at 400° F for 30 minutes, basting with juices several times. Test fish with fork to see if it flakes. When done sprinkle with parsley and serve with pan juice and lime wedges. Makes 4 to 6 servings.

Bluefish Baked with Stuffing

Many people feel bluefish is strong flavored. However, this fine fish can be cooked in any number of ways to enhance and, if you will, disguise its flavor. Bluefish Baked with Stuffing is one.

> 1 cup soft white bread crumbs
> 1 chopped green onion
> 3 tablespoons chopped cooked peeled shrimp
> 2 tablespoons chopped fresh parsley
> 4 tablespoons melted butter or margarine
> ⅛ teaspoon ground thyme
> 1 tablespoon fresh lemon juice
> 2 pounds boneless bluefish fillets, cut in 4 servings
> ½ cup fine dry bread crumbs

Mix soft bread crumbs with onion, shrimp, parsley, butter, thyme, and lemon juice.

Check fillets for bones, then place skin side down in a buttered flat baking dish. Spread bread mixture equally on fillets and sprinkle with dry bread crumbs. Bake at 350° F for 30 minutes. Makes 4 servings.

Bluefish Tartar

Serve Bluefish Tartar with cooked rice, asparagus tips, lettuce and tomato with oil and vinegar, and for dessert strawberries.

1½ pounds bluefish fillets
2 tablespoons lemon juice
½ cup tartar sauce
3 tablespoons buttermilk
2 tablespoons chopped fresh parsley
Salt and freshly ground pepper to taste

Arrange fillets in a buttered baking dish. Sprinkle with lemon juice. Mix tartar sauce with buttermilk, parsley, salt, and pepper.

Spread over fillets. Bake at 375° F for 20 to 25 minutes or until fish flakes easily. Makes 4 servings.

Bluefish with Sour Cream Dill Sauce

With this tasty bluefish serve whipped potatoes, buttered peas and carrots, and hot rolls. Apple and grape salad makes a salad-dessert.

2 pounds bluefish fillets
3 tablespoons lemon juice
½ cup dairy sour cream
¼ cup mayonnaise
1 green onion, chopped
2 tablespoons snipped fresh dill
Freshly ground pepper to taste

Combine fish fillets with lemon juice and allow to stand in refrigerator for at least an hour. Drain and place in a buttered flat baking dish.

Mix sour cream with mayonnaise, onion, dill, and pepper. Spread over fish in pan. Bake at 400° F for 30 minutes. If desired, run under broiler to brown slightly. Makes 4 servings.

ENTREES

Cape Cod Turkey

It doesn't take long for any of us who are not natives of Cape Cod to learn that Cape Cod Turkey is codfish with egg sauce. This recipe would give the turkey a run for its money.

2 to 3 pounds boneless cod fillets
Salt and freshly ground pepper to taste
4 tablespoons melted butter or margarine
4 cups fresh bread crumbs
1 tablespoon grated onion
1 teaspoon each dried dill weed and dried leaf thyme, crushed
2 tablespoons chopped parsley
1 egg, beaten
2 tablespoons melted butter or margarine

Sprinkle fillets with salt and pepper and place half of fillets in a well-buttered baking dish, about 12 × 8 × 2 inches. Make a stuffing by combining 4 tablespoons butter with crumbs, onion, and herbs. Mix lightly to blend flavors, then stir in egg. Spread stuffing on cod fillets in dish. Cover with remaining fillets and spread with 2 tablespoons melted butter. Bake at 350° F for 35 to 40 minutes or until fish flakes easily with a fork. Serve with Egg Sauce, below. Makes 6 servings.

Egg Sauce

Combine ¼ cup butter or margarine, ⅓ cup all-purpose flour, 1 teaspoon dry mustard, ½ teaspoon salt, and freshly ground pepper to taste in a 2-quart saucepan. Cook and stir over medium heat for 2 minutes. Gradually add 3 cups milk and continue cooking and stirring until mixture boils and is thickened. Add 4 peeled and chopped hard-cooked eggs and 2 tablespoons chopped fresh parsley. Serve with codfish.

Creamed Salt Cod

Creamed salt codfish was a basic Cape dish at one time. Salt codfish was a Cape product, and about the only fish cheaper were cod tongues and cheeks. With the advocacy of lower salt in the diet and the increase in price of salt cod, it has lost some of its popularity — though I must say, a few years back I went to a church supper where creamed salt codfish was the star of the menu and it was mighty tasty. At any rate, a Cape Cod seafood cookbook wouldn't be complete without a recipe for creamed salt cod.

1 pound salt codfish
Water
¼ cup butter or margarine
¼ cup flour
3 cups milk
Mashed potatoes for 4

Soak codfish in water, changing water often depending on the saltiness of the cod, for at least 3 hours. Drain. Cover cod with boiling water in a large skillet or saucepan. Simmer below boiling until cod flakes easily with a fork. Drain. Add butter and flour and stir in milk. Cook and stir until mixture boils and is thickened. Serve over hot mashed potatoes. Makes 4 servings.

Variation: For a delicious creamed salt cod substitute, use 1 to 1½ pounds regular codfish (boneless) instead of the salt cod in this recipe. Omit all the soaking, of course, and poach cod in a small amount of water until it flakes. Drain and proceed.

Potatoes Stuffed with Codfish

A hearty combination of potatoes and fish that is a Cape favorite. It is good with or without Pork Gravy.

> 4 large baking potatoes
> 1½ pounds boneless codfish (or other fish fillets)
> 2 cups boiling water
> 1 cup hot milk (about)
> ¼ cup butter or margarine
> 1½ teaspoons grated onion
> 1½ tablespoons chopped fresh parsley
> 1½ teaspoons Dijon style mustard
> Salt and freshly ground pepper to taste
> Paprika

Scrub and oil baking potatoes and prick one or two places with a fork. Bake at 400° F for 50 to 60 minutes or until tender when pinched between two fingers.

While potatoes are baking poach fish in water to cover, just below boiling point, for 5 to 8 minutes or until it flakes easily with a fork. Drain and flake fish, saving the liquid. Remove any bones from fish if necessary.

Cut tops from baked potatoes and scoop out insides, leaving shells about ¼ inch thick. Reserve shells. Beat potato flesh with milk (and some poaching liquid if needed for texture), butter, onion, parsley, mustard, salt, and pepper until light and fluffy. Stir in fish. Pile lightly into potato shells and sprinkle with paprika. Bake at 350° F for 25 to 30 minutes until hot. Serve with Pork Gravy (below) if desired. Makes 4 servings.

Pork Gravy

¼ pound bacon or salt pork, minced
¼ cup all-purpose flour
1½ cups reserved fish liquid
¾ cup milk

Cook bacon or pork in a saucepan until lightly browned. Remove bacon (or pork) and all but 2 tablespoons of drippings. Add flour to drippings. Cook and stir for 2 minutes. Gradually stir in fish liquid and milk and cook until thickened, stirring. Stir in bacon or pork. Serve with baked stuffed potatoes. Makes about 2 cups.

Saucy Cod Fillets

Served with buttered new potatoes and peas, these fillets make a delicious and easily prepared meal. The vermouth gives the codfish a piquant flavor.

2 pounds boneless cod fillets
¼ cup melted butter or margarine
2 tablespoons fresh lemon juice
Salt and freshly ground pepper to taste
¼ cup dry vermouth
3 green onions, finely chopped
1 cup mayonnaise
1½ teaspoons chopped fresh dill or ½ teaspoon dried
    dill, crushed

Arrange fillets in a buttered 9 × 13-inch dish which can be used under broiler. Spread with butter and sprinkle with lemon juice, salt, and pepper. Broil 4 inches from source of heat for 5 minutes, turning once if fillets are thick. Mix remaining ingredients and spread over fish. Broil 2 to 3 minutes longer or until sauce is lightly browned. Makes 4 servings.

Elegant Codfish Casserole

This casserole will star in your repertoire of fish recipes. Serve with it rice amandine, steamed Chinese peas, celery slaw, cranberry sauce, and cheese and crackers.

> 2½ pounds boneless cod fillets
> 1 can (10½ ounces) condensed cream of shrimp soup
> ½ cup margarine, melted
> 1 teaspoon Worcestershire sauce
> 1 teaspoon lemon juice
> Dash Tabasco sauce
> 30 crushed crackers (use ½ Ritz and ½ unsalted single
>   soda crackers)
> 2 teaspoons chopped parsley

Cut fillets into serving size pieces and place in a buttered flat casserole. Spread soup on top. Bake at 375° F for 15 minutes. While fish is baking mix remaining ingredients. Spread over fish in casserole and continue baking for 8 to 10 minutes or until fish flakes easily with a fork. Makes 4 or 5 servings.

Broiled Dogfish with Tomato Sauce

Dogfish are small relatives of the shark and are disliked by fishermen because they tend to feed on more appetizing fish — appetizing at least in name. If you have ever eaten fish and chips in England the chances are that you have eaten dogfish, as that is the primary fish used for that delicacy. It is an excellently flavored fish and it is sad that more of it is not used in this country as a food fish. With Broiled Dogfish with Tomato Sauce try French fried potatoes, a salad of boiled mixed vegetables, and jelly roll with strawberry sauce for dessert.

> 2 large dogfish fillets (about 2 pounds)
> Softened butter or margarine
> Salt and freshly ground pepper to taste
> 1 can (8 ounces) tomato sauce
> ¼ cup lemon juice

Spread dogfish with softened butter and season with salt and pepper. Place in an oiled fish grill. Mix tomato sauce and lemon juice.

Cook fish 4 inches from source of heat in an oven broiler or over hot coals in a charcoal grill. Baste fish lightly with sauce as it cooks. Cook 5 minutes on one side, turn, and cook 4 minutes on other side or until fish flakes easily with a fork. Serve with any leftover sauce. Makes 4 servings.

Fried Eel

Just to mention the word eel makes many people wince, but a tastier morsel is hard to find. Eels are quite plentiful here in Cape waters. They inhabit both fresh and salt water, and while they can be caught all year, in winter they tend to hibernate in the mud and are more difficult to find. You do not often see them in fish markets because of the prejudice against them. Scandinavians consider eels a delicacy, however, and being of partly Scandinavian descent I can remember smoked eel as a holiday treat.

Eels take about 15 years to develop into the form we know. They have an interesting history. Their eggs are spawned and fertilized deep in the Sargasso Sea — the heart of the Devil's Triangle off Bermuda. Shortly they develop into transparent larvae that resemble willow leaves. During this time the whims of the ocean currents distribute the willow-like larvae from the Gulf of Mexico to Northern Canadian provinces. At the end of about a year they change into elvers — baby eel — and start spring migration into their freshwater habitats, often going miles over dry land to get there.*

When you can find eels in the fish market they will be cleaned. But if you are given fresh-caught eels you will need to do the cleaning. Nail the head of the eel to a board. Slit the skin completely around the neck. Peel back, and pull off with pliers just like a sock. Slit the belly to remove the guts, cut off the head, and the eel is ready to cook. I'm like the raccoon, I wash everything before I eat or cook it, so I'd recommend washing the eel after its cleaning.

Cut into serving size pieces, about 2 inches. Dip in lemon juice; roll in flour; season with salt and freshly ground pepper; and fry in butter, oil, or bacon fat until nicely browned all over. Serve with lemon wedges if you like.

*Information from The Institute for Anguilliform Research and Mariculture.

Broiled Eel

Here is a recipe for just plain broiled eel. French fried potatoes, steamed green beans and onion, mixed greens, hot bread, and fresh fruit will make the meal.

2 or 3 pounds eel
Salt and freshly ground pepper to taste
Olive oil
Lemon juice
Chopped fresh parsley
Lemon wedges

Clean eel, if necessary, and cut into 2-inch pieces. Sprinkle with salt and pepper and brush with oil. Broil about 4 inches from heat source, turning to brown both sides, for about 5 minutes or until flesh flakes when separated with fork. Sprinkle cooked eel with lemon juice and parsley. Serve with lemon wedges. Makes 4 servings.

Eel in Beer Sauce

This is a way to serve eel that will probably fool friends if you don't give it away. Serve it with rice or noodles, buttered carrots, and pine-apple and cottage cheese salad.

3 tablespoons butter or margarine
2 tablespoons flour
1½ cups stale beer
1 bay leaf
1 clove
2 tablespoons lemon juice
3 tablespoons minced onion
1 tablespoon chopped fresh parsley
2 eels, cleaned and cut into 2-inch pieces
Salt and freshly ground pepper to taste
Chopped parsley to garnish

Heat butter in medium saucepan. Add flour and cook and stir for 2 minutes. Stir in beer and cook and stir until thickened. Tie bay leaf and clove in a piece of cheesecloth and add with remaining ingredients to beer sauce. Cover and simmer about 30 minutes. Remove bay leaf and clove. Season to taste with salt and pepper. Serve sprinkled with additional chopped parsley. Makes 4 servings.

Grilled Eel with Caper Sauce

It is easiest to make the Caper Sauce first and keep it hot or reheat it. Steamed snow peas, fresh spinach and mushroom salad, and lemon pie are good partners for the eel.

> 2 eels, cleaned
> Lemon juice
> Flour
> Steamed rice or cooked noodles

Cut eels into 4-inch pieces, remove backbone, and dip in lemon juice, then in flour. Broil 4 inches from heat source until flesh flakes when separated with fork, about 3 to 4 minutes. Serve eel and Caper Sauce (below) with rice or noodles. Makes 4 servings.

Caper Sauce

> 3 tablespoons butter or margarine
> 3 tablespoons flour
> ½ teaspoon salt
> Freshly ground pepper to taste
> 1½ cups half-and-half
> 3 tablespoons chopped capers*

Melt butter in saucepan, add 3 tablespoons flour, and cook 2 minutes. Add salt and pepper and stir in half-and-half. Cook and stir until mixture boils and is thickened. Add capers and simmer 5 minutes.

*If capers are salted type, rinse well before using.

Spanish Hake

Spanish Hake is a meal-in-one-dish. A tossed salad and hot rolls would go well with this delicious recipe. Fresh fruit makes a good dessert.

    1½ to 2 pounds hake steaks
    Flour seasoned with salt, pepper, and paprika
    4 tablespoons olive oil
    1 clove garlic, finely chopped
    2 cups diced carrots
    ¼ cup uncooked rice
    1 cup green shrimp, shelled and deveined
    ½ cup chopped raw clams
    ¼ cup chopped fresh parsley
    Salt and freshly ground pepper to taste
    1¼ cups dry white wine
    4 tablespoons lemon juice
    ¾ cup clam juice

Dip steaks in seasoned flour. Heat oil in a skillet large enough to hold fish steaks and all ingredients to come. Add garlic and fish, and brown fish on both sides. Add remaining ingredients. Bring to simmer, cover, and cook for about 15 minutes. Makes 4 servings.

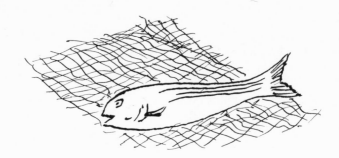

Breaded Baked Hake

With Breaded Baked Hake serve stewed canned tomatoes, steamed broccoli, celery slaw, and apple sauce with cookies for dessert. Other fish fillets such as cusk and tautog can also be baked in this manner.

3 medium onions
3 pounds hake fillets
1 cup dry bread crumbs
1 teaspoon salt
Freshly ground pepper to taste
½ teaspoon paprika
¼ teaspoon ground thyme
¼ teaspoon celery salt
1 tablespoon parsley flakes
6 tablespoons butter or margarine
1 cup water
6 tablespoons lemon juice

Chop onions coarsely (there should be enough to make a half-inch layer) and spread in a buttered baking dish large enough to hold hake. Lay hake on onions. Mix crumbs and seasonings; spread on fish. Dot with butter. Sprinkle ½ cup of the water and 3 tablespoons of the lemon juice over crumbs. Bake at 375° F for 15 minutes. Sprinkle with remaining ½ cup water and 3 tablespoons lemon juice and bake another 15 minutes or until crumbs are browned. Be sure to have some onions with each serving of hake and crumbs. Makes 6 servings.

Baked Mackerel with Tarragon Sauce

If you are one of those who object to mackerel because it has a "strong" taste, try it with this Tarragon Sauce. Prepare the sauce the day before and refrigerate to blend the flavors.

2 pounds boneless fillets of mackerel
2 or 3 slices bacon

Put mackerel in buttered baking dish and top with bacon slices. Bake at 350° F about 30 minutes. Serve with cold Tarragon Sauce, below. Makes 4 servings.

Tarragon Sauce

2 tablespoons tarragon vinegar
2 tablespoons cider vinegar
½ cup olive oil
½ teaspoon each salt and paprika
Freshly ground pepper to taste
2 tablespoons each chopped green pepper and chopped
  celery
2 sweet gherkins chopped
1 teaspoon chopped chives

Mix all ingredients and chill overnight. Makes about 1 cup.

Monkfish in Mushroom Sauce

Monkfish, also known as goosefish, is found in waters from Newfound-
land to North Carolina. It is an ugly fish with an enormous mouth and
a head which is grotesquely out of proportion to the rest of the body.
The tail portion is sold as steaks or fillets. The flesh is white and has a
firm texture when cooked. With Monkfish in Mushroom Sauce serve
a green vegetable and baby carrots, romaine with buttermilk dressing,
and for dessert half grapefruits.

1½ pounds monkfish
2 cans (10¾ ounces each) condensed cream of
  mushroom soup
½ cup milk or light cream
⅓ cup sherry
½ pound fresh mushrooms, sliced
1 small onion, finely chopped
4 baked puff pastry shells

Cut monkfish into bite-size pieces, removing any membrane that
may be present. In a large saucepan blend soup, milk, and sherry. Heat
soup, stirring constantly. Add fish, mushroom slices, and onion. Cook,
covered, over low heat until fish turns white and flakes about 10 minutes, stirring often. Serve in baked puff pastry shells. Makes 4 servings.

Baked Ocean Catfish Yogurt

Ocean catfish, also called wolf fish in some markets, is one of my favorite fish. Whenever it is in the fish market I buy as much as I have room for in my freezer and freeze it in individual portions. It is a white-fleshed fish with a delicate flavor. It can be used in any recipe calling for cod or haddock. With Baked Ocean Catfish Yogurt serve whipped potatoes, chopped broccoli, orange and onion salad on chopped lettuce, and chocolate-covered ice cream bars for dessert.

1 green pepper, seeded and sliced
1 onion, sliced
1 tomato, sliced
2 pounds ocean catfish fillets
¼ teaspoon salt
Freshly ground pepper to taste
¼ cup tomato juice
2 tablespoons butter or margarine
⅛ teaspoon paprika
1 cup plain yogurt

Place half of the vegetables in a buttered baking dish.

Season fish fillets with salt and pepper to taste and arrange on top of vegetables. Cover with remaining vegetables. Add tomato juice. Dot with butter and sprinkle with salt, pepper, and paprika. Bake at 350° F for 15 minutes or until fish is almost tender. Cover with yogurt and return to oven until yogurt is bubbly and heated through. Makes 4 servings.

Foil Baked Pollock

The packages for Foil Baked Pollock can be prepared in advance and refrigerated until ready to bake. If this is done allow about 5 minutes extra baking time. Serve with mashed squash, mixed vegetables, and tossed salad. For dessert prepare baked apples.

> Heavy duty aluminum foil
> 1 envelope dry onion soup mix
> 2 pounds boneless fillets of pollock, cut into 4 serving
> pieces
> 4 teaspoons butter or margarine
> 4 tablespoons chopped fresh parsley

Cut heavy duty foil into 4 9×12-inch rectangles. On each rectangle sprinkle 2 tablespoons soup mix. Place fish over soup mix and divide remaining mix among fish. Put a teaspoon of butter and a tablespoon of chopped parsley on each fish piece. Fold foil over fish and seal tightly. Place packages on a baking sheet, seam side down, and bake at 400° F for about 15 minutes, turning once. Open one package to see that the fish flakes easily with a fork. The fish can be removed from the foil to serve or served on the plate in the package. Makes 4 servings.

Sauteed Fish Roe

Roe is the eggs of the fish. Shad roe has always been considered a special delicacy, but other fish roes are marvelously flavored and (in season) much less expensive than shad. Herring roe is widely available in the spring. Cod and haddock roe are in the market about the same time.

One of my friends, who has a busy fish market, told me of a couple who had made a custom of having shad roe and champagne for brunch every Saturday. In season, my friend froze enough shad roe so she could provide it for them all year round.

1½ pounds (about) fish roe
¼ to ⅓ cup milk
¼ cup flour
Salt and freshly ground pepper to taste
4 tablespoons butter
2 tablespoons fresh lemon juice

Put roe into milk in a flat pan. Dip in flour to cover and season to taste. Heat butter in a large skillet and cook roe over medium heat 5 to 8 minutes, covered. Turn to continue cooking at the halfway point. When done roe will be firm to the touch. Serve roe with butter from skillet and lemon juice. Makes 4 servings.

Many people like to serve roe with scrambled eggs for breakfast. If you are having this combination, about 1 pound of roe should be sufficient for 4.

Deviled Roe

Serve this unusual dish as a party canape or as a first course with tomato juice. Any kind of roe can be used.

Parboil roe in water seasoned with 1 tablespoon vinegar and 1 teaspoon salt per quart water. Pierce sacs with a sharp knife point in several places before parboiling so they will not explode. Simmer small sacs of roe below boiling point 7 to 8 minutes; simmer larger sacs (from 3 to 5 pound fish) about 15 minutes.

Mash parboiled roe, and for each 1 cup mashed roe mix in 1 tablespoon melted butter, 2 teaspoons Worcestershire sauce, salt and freshly ground pepper to taste, and 1 teaspoon Dijon style mustard.

Spread on lightly toasted bread and place in a 400° F oven for 5 minutes. Cut each slice in squares to serve.

Roe Parmesan

Any kind of roe in season can be used for this dish. Shad roe is usually the first kind to come to mind, but all fish roe is good and should not be spurned. This recipe for Roe Parmesan will make a light supper. Serve with creamed peas, tiny new potatoes, and sliced tomatoes dressed with oil and vinegar.

2 large fish roe
Salt and freshly ground pepper to taste
3 tablespoons melted butter
½ cup grated Parmesan cheese

Place roe in a buttered baking dish. Pierce several places with the point of a knife. Sprinkle with salt and pepper to taste and pour melted butter over roe. Cover with grated Parmesan cheese. Bake at 375° F for 25 to 30 minutes. Makes 2 servings.

Baked Salmon with Rosemary

Salmon is a fine fish for steaks; but swordfish has always been associated with Cape Cod while salmon was an interloper from the West.

This recipe uses a piece of salmon large enough for a party. Scalloped potatoes, steamed green beans and celery, sliced ripe tomatoes, and hot French bread could make the menu complete. For dessert serve a tart sherbet with crisp cookies.

> 5-pound piece of salmon
> Juice of 1 lemon
> 1 teaspoon crushed dried rosemary
> 2 to 3 tablespoons softened butter
> ¼ cup dry white wine
> Chopped fresh parsley
> Lemon wedges

Lay fish on heavy foil in a flat baking pan. Sprinkle inside with lemon juice and rosemary. Spread outside with softened butter. Bake at 375° F for 30 to 40 minutes or until fish flakes, basting with wine and pan juices.

To serve, use foil as a holder to remove fish to platter. Remove skin from fish and cut and remove foil. Sprinkle fish with parsley and decorate with lemon wedges. Makes about 10 servings.

Coulibiak of Salmon

This dish is of Russian origin and is not as complicated as it sounds once you have made it. For a seafood buffet it is beautiful to look at and even better to eat.

1 cup water
1 cup dry white wine
8 peppercorns
2 or 3 onion slices
3 salmon steaks (about 1½ pounds)
½ cup uncooked long-grain rice
3 tablespoons butter
1 cup chopped fresh mushrooms
1½ tablespoons chopped fresh dill or 1½ teaspoons dried, crushed
1 package (17¼ ounces) frozen prerolled puff pastry sheets
1 egg yolk, beaten
½ cup melted butter
Parsley sprigs

Combine water, wine, peppercorns, and onion slices in a skillet and simmer covered for 15 minutes. Add salmon steaks and cook below boiling point for about 5 minutes or until fish flakes easily. Remove fish from liquid and cool. When cooled take out any bones and skin and flake coarsely.

Strain liquid from fish and add water, if necessary, to make 1½ cups. Add rice, 1 tablespoon of the butter, and ¼ teaspoon salt and bring to a boil in a heavy saucepan. Stir with a fork and cook, covered, 12 to 14 minutes over low heat. Drain excess liquid, if necessary.

Heat remaining 2 tablespoons of butter and saute mushrooms with dill for 5 minutes. Mix with cooked rice. Cool.

To assemble: Defrost 2 sheets of puff pastry for 10 minutes. Roll one between wax paper sheets that are 1 inch larger than the pastry both lengthwise and crosswise. Transfer to a greased baking pan with raised edges. (A jelly roll pan will do nicely.) Pile half the rice mixture on the pastry to within one inch of the edge. Pile cooked salmon evenly over the rice and spread remaining rice on top. Roll a second pastry sheet in wax paper in the same way. Carefully transfer over rice and salmon.

Moisten underside of edges of top pastry sheet with egg yolk and seal bottom and top sheets together, crimping to make a pretty edge. Cut three ½-inch holes in top and brush all over with egg yolk. Bake at 350° F for 45 minutes or until golden. Transfer to serving platter and pour melted butter into holes in top. Garnish with parsley. Slice to serve. Makes 4 servings as a main dish, more in a buffet.

Boston Scrod a la King

Cape Codders have long had an affair with creamed fish. Boston Scrod a la King is a fancy recipe for creamed fish. Serve it with mashed potatoes for the full effect. Scrod is young cod or haddock.

2 pounds scrod
Melted butter for brushing
¼ cup butter or margarine
¼ cup flour
Salt and freshly ground pepper to taste
2 cups milk
1 cup sliced fresh mushrooms
1 green pepper, slivered
1 tablespoon vegetable oil
¼ cup dry sherry
½ cup thinly sliced pimiento

Scrod: Cut 2 pounds scrod into serving size pieces. Broil about 4 inches from source of heat for 5 minutes on each side, brushing with melted butter, until fish flakes easily with fork.

Sauce: Melt ¼ cup butter in a saucepan and blend in flour, salt, and pepper. Cook and stir for 2 minutes. Gradually add milk and stir over medium heat until thickened and smooth. Cook mushrooms and green pepper in vegetable oil until mushrooms are lightly browned. Add with remaining ingredients to sauce. Hold over low heat, covered, to blend flavors for about 5 minutes.

Serve scrod covered with a la king sauce. Makes 4 servings.

Baked Smelt

Smelts are generally a good buy and have fine flavor. If they are not cleaned, it is no problem. Just slit the belly, take out the guts, and wash well. Cut off the head or not, as pleases you. (Most fish markets will clean smelts if you ask them to.) Allow 4 to 6 smelts per person depending on size.

Tiny parsleyed buttered potatoes, steamed snow peas, romaine and onion salad, and for dessert sliced bananas and strawberries will taste good with Baked Smelt.

16 to 24 smelts, depending on size
1 medium onion, sliced
4 slices bacon
½ cup fresh chopped mushrooms
½ cup dry white wine
Freshly ground pepper to taste

Clean smelt, if necessary. Remove heads, if desired.

Place onion slices in bottom of well-buttered baking dish and place smelts on onion. Cook bacon partially in skillet. Remove and place over smelts. Saute mushrooms in remaining bacon fat and add wine while scraping skillet with spoon to get any crusted bits from bottom. Pour mushrooms and wine over fish. Sprinkle with pepper to taste. Bake at 400° F for about 25 minutes. Makes 4 servings.

This recipe can also be used for herring.

Sole with Yogurt Sauce

When you are baking thin fillets such as sole it is a smart trick to fold them into thirds or halves. This gives the fillets a little more bulk and they are not as likely to dry out. Buttered noodles, steamed celery and green beans, tossed salad, and frozen eclairs would be my suggestions for serving with Sole with Yogurt Sauce.

2 pounds sole fillets
2 tablespoons prepared horseradish
2 tablespoons Dijon style mustard
¼ cup lemon juice
⅔ cup plain yogurt
¼ cup butter, softened
2 to 3 tablespoons chopped parsley

Fold fillets into thirds and place in a shallow baking dish. Mix together the remaining ingredients and spread over fish. Bake at 400° F for 25 minutes or until fish flakes. Makes 4 servings.

Noodle Casserole Supreme

Don't count the calories when preparing this main dish.

½ pound narrow egg noodles
½ cup butter or margarine
¾ pound fillets of sole
⅔ cup dry white wine
1 green onion, finely chopped
1 cup light cream
½ cup mayonnaise
¼ teaspoon salt
Dash Tabasco sauce
2 teaspoons lemon juice
⅓ pound cooked shrimp, peeled and deveined
6 tablespoons grated Parmesan cheese

Cook noodles in boiling salted water for 8 to 9 minutes. Drain, cool slightly, and mix with one tablespoon of the butter. Set aside.

Cut sole into 1-inch squares and put into skillet with wine, onion, and 2 tablespoons of the butter. Simmer 3 minutes. Remove fish to a bowl. Cook liquid until reduced by half. Strain. Add cream, mayonnaise, salt, and Tabasco to liquid and whisk until smooth. Stir in lemon juice.

Chop shrimp finely and mix with fish. Melt remaining butter.

In a buttered 2-quart casserole alternate layers of noodles with fish and shrimp mixture, Parmesan cheese, and sauce, ending with noodles and Parmesan cheese. Pour melted butter over all. Bake at 400° F for 30 to 35 minutes or until lightly browned and bubbly. Makes 4 servings.

Baked Swordfish Steak

Swordfish is the king of the fish that cut well into steaks. It is a toss-up whether my off-Cape friends prefer swordfish or lobster when they visit here.

Swordfish can be baked (as in this recipe), charcoal broiled, or broiled in the range broiler. It is one fish that I would not pan fry if facilities for the other cooking methods were available. All swordfish recipes can also be prepared with Mako shark or salmon.

With Baked Swordfish Steak put 4 potatoes in the oven to bake about 35 minutes before the fish. Steamed broccoli, watercress salad, and fresh or frozen sliced peaches can complete the dinner.

2 pounds swordfish steak, 1 inch thick
Cooking oil
Flour seasoned with salt, pepper, and paprika
½ cup finely chopped onion
2 tablespoons chopped fresh dill (or more to taste)
4 tablespoons melted butter
½ cup dry white wine

Dip steaks in cooking oil and then in seasoned flour. Place steaks in one layer in an oiled flat baking pan. Sprinkle with onions, dill, and melted butter. Pour wine around fish.

Bake at 400° F for 20 to 25 minutes or until fish flakes easily, basting twice with wine. Serve fish with pan sauce. Makes 4 servings.

Stuffed Tautog

Tautog or blackfish is a North American coastal fish. It is very abundant but almost ignored as a food fish. It has an excellent flavor and can be baked, broiled, or used for chowder.

For stuffing, as in this recipe, about a 5-pound tautog will be satisfactory. The fish can be gutted and skinned or scaled. Make cuts through the skin near the head, down through the skin alongside the dorsal fin from head to tail, and along the ventral fin back to the tail. At this point you can pull the skin off using pliers. Remove head, tail, and fins and wash fish well. It is now ready to stuff.

1 tautog, 5 to 6 pounds, cleaned whole and skinned or
    scaled
3 tablespoons butter or margarine, softened
2 cups bread stuffing (below)
6 to 8 lemon slices
6 stuffed olives, sliced

Rub the fish with 2 tablespoons of the softened butter. Fill cavity with stuffing. Arrange fish on a piece of heavy aluminum foil in a shallow pan. Bake at 325° F for about 25 minutes or until fish flakes easily with fork, basting with remaining butter. Carefully lift fish out of pan with aluminum foil and place on platter. Pull foil out from under fish and garnish with lemon slices and olives. Makes about 6 servings.

Bread Stuffing

Prepare 2 cups commercial bread stuffing as directed on package. Or saute ¼ cup chopped onion and ½ cup chopped celery in ¼ cup butter. Add 2 cups toasted bread cubes, ½ teaspoon poultry seasoning, 2 tablespoons lemon juice, and salt and freshly ground pepper to taste. Mix well and use to stuff fish.

Tautog with Snappy Cheese

Tautog with Snappy Cheese goes well with French fried potatoes, steamed sliced celery and onions, Boston lettuce with oil and vinegar, hot bread, and brick ice cream.

2 pounds fillet of tautog
¼ cup melted butter or margarine
Salt and freshly ground pepper to taste
1 cup grated Cheddar cheese
¼ cup chili sauce
1½ tablespoons Dijon style mustard
1 tablespoon prepared horseradish

Place fillets on greased broiler pan. Brush with melted butter and season to taste with salt and pepper. Broil 4 inches from source of heat 8 to 10 minutes or until fish flakes easily with a fork.

Blend cheese, chili sauce, mustard, and horseradish. Spread over fish and return to broiler for 1 to 2 minutes for cheese to melt and brown lightly. Makes 4 servings.

Baked Tautog with Dill

Serve mashed potatoes with Baked Tautog with Dill; also buttered carrots, raw spinach salad, hot rolls, and pineapple slices to finish the menu.

2 pounds tautog fillets
3 tablespoons minced parsley
3 sprigs fresh dill, minced
3 tablespoons butter or margarine
3 tablespoons flour
1⅓ cups water or fish stock
Salt and freshly ground pepper to taste
1 egg yolk
Paprika

Put tautog fillets in a buttered baking dish and sprinkle with parsley and dill.

Melt butter in saucepan and stir in flour. Let cook 2 minutes. Gradually stir in water and cook and stir until mixture boils and is thickened. Season to taste. Pour over fish in baking dish. Bake at 375° F for 30 minutes or until fish flakes easily. Remove fish to a warm platter. Beat egg yolk into sauce in baking dish. Pour over fish and sprinkle with paprika.
Makes 4 servings.

Whiting with Mayonnaise Sauce

The lemony flavor and creamy texture of mayonnaise goes well with many fish. You will like this whiting recipe. Steamed potatoes, fresh spinach, a salad of lettuce and grapefruit sections, cookies, and tea fill out the dinner menu.

4 whiting, about 1½ pounds each
Salt and freshly ground pepper to taste
1 medium onion, thinly sliced
2 slices bacon
⅔ cups mayonnaise
1 tablespoon chopped green olives
2 teaspoons prepared horseradish
1 tablespoon lemon juice

Clean whiting, leaving head on if desired. Remove fins and gills. Place in a well-buttered flat baking pan and season to taste with salt and pepper. Cover fish with thin onion slices and bacon slices cut in half. Bake at 375° F for about 25 minutes or until fish flakes easily.
While fish is baking, mix mayonnaise with remaining ingredients. Spread over baked fish and run under the broiler for 2 to 3 minutes to brown. Makes 4 servings.

Whiting in Foil

One of the advantages of cooking in foil is that the foil packages can be put together in advance and brought out to cook at the last minute. This enables you to get everything else ready. With Whiting in Foil I might serve hashed brown potatoes; zucchini and tomatoes cooked together; whole-wheat rolls; raw celery, carrots, and radishes; and cherry pie.

3 green onions, chopped
8 small whole mushrooms
1 tablespoon honey
½ cup dry white wine
½ cup oil
2 tablespoons chopped parsley
⅛ teaspoon ground cumin
½ teaspoon salt
Freshly ground pepper to taste
4 cleaned small whiting (about 1½ pounds each)

Combine onions, mushrooms, honey, wine, oil, parsley, and seasonings. Add whiting and marinate, covered, in the refrigerator for several hours.

To cook, remove fish and mushrooms from marinade and place each fish and 2 mushrooms along with a spoonful of the marinade on a piece of heavy duty foil about 17 × 10 inches. Wrap foil around fish, sealing well, and cook on grill about 8 minutes on each side, depending on how hot the coals are. Or bake fish in foil in a 400° F oven 20–25 minutes. Makes 4 servings.

Fish with Curried Tomatoes

Curry is a flavor that goes well with fish. Here it is combined with tomatoes in a sauce. Serve buttered rice, a tossed green salad, steamed green beans, and hot rolls with this recipe.

ENTREES

2 tablespoons butter or margarine
1 medium onion, chopped
½ cup chopped fresh tomatoes
1 short celery stalk, chopped
½ teaspoon curry powder
2 tablespoons lemon juice
½ teaspoon salt
Freshly ground pepper to taste
1 pound fish fillets (cod, haddock, ocean perch, hake)

Heat butter in small pan and cook onion, tomatoes, and celery until tender. Add curry, lemon juice, salt, and pepper.

Broil fish fillets 4 inches from source of heat about 6 minutes, depending on thickness. Spread with sauce and broil 1 or 2 minutes longer. Makes 2 servings.

Broiled Fish with Shrimp Sauce

Very often plain broiled fish looks too plain. Add shrimp sauce to the fish and it becomes a completely new dish without adding too many extra calories.

2 pounds fish fillets (flounder, sole, or ocean catfish)
2 tablespoons lemon juice
1 tablespoon butter or margarine
4 tablespoons chopped Spanish onions
2 tablespoons chopped fresh parsley
½ teaspoon dried rosemary, crushed
¼ cup dry white wine
½ cup tiny shrimp, cooked and peeled, defrosted
 if frozen

Arrange fillets in 4 portions on a buttered broiling tray and sprinkle with lemon juice.

Heat butter in small skillet and saute onions until tender. Add parsley, rosemary, and wine and cook for 2 to 3 minutes. Add shrimp and cook for 1 or 2 minutes longer.

Meanwhile, broil fish 4 inches from source of heat for 6 to 8 minutes, depending on thickness of fillets, or until fish flakes easily with a fork. Arrange fillets on a serving platter and divide sauce over fillets. Makes 4 servings.

Fish Fillets Parmesan

The flavorful sauce and Parmesan cheese make these easy rolled fillets a favorite dish. Heat French fries in the oven while the fish is baking. Complete the menu with fresh or frozen asparagus tips, romaine lettuce and orange sections with a mildly flavored salad dressing, and Italian bread.

> 2 pounds boneless fillets of fish (cod, flounder, sole, hake, ocean catfish)
> ½ cup melted butter or margarine
> 3 tablespoons lemon juice
> 1 teaspoon grated onion
> Dash Tabasco sauce
> ½ cup grated Parmesan cheese

Roll fillets and place side by side in baking dish that just holds fish. Mix butter with lemon juice, onion, and Tabasco. Pour evenly over fish. Sprinkle with cheese. Bake at 375° F for 25 to 30 minutes or until fish flakes easily with fork. Serve with sauce from pan. Makes 4 servings.

Fish Fillets with Curried Mayonnaise

Any thin white-fleshed fish fillets can be used for this recipe. Add tomato juice, grapefruit orange salad, hot French bread, and ice cream for dessert.

> ½ cup mayonnaise
> 1 teaspoon curry powder (or more to taste)
> ¼ teaspoon salt
> ¼ teaspoon ginger
> 2 tablespoons chopped chives
> 1½ pounds fish fillets
> 4 tablespoons butter or margarine, melted
> ½ cup fine dry bread crumbs

Combine mayonnaise with curry, salt, ginger, and chives.

Arrange fillets in 4 serving portions on a well-greased broiler rack. Spread with 2 tablespoons melted butter and broil 4 inches from source of heat for 3 minutes. Remove from broiler. Spread fillets with mayonnaise and sprinkle with bread crumbs. Drizzle with remaining butter. Return to broiler and broil 3 to 4 minutes longer or until crumbs begin to brown. Makes 4 servings.

Fish Fillets with Tomato Sauce

In the summer, when luscious ripe red tomatoes are available, prepare this fish and tomato dish for family and friends.

> 2 pounds boneless fish fillets (flounder, cod, haddock, or ocean perch)
> Salt and freshly ground pepper to taste
> 1 egg, beaten
> 2 tablespoons melted butter or margarine
> 1½ cups fine fresh bread crumbs
> 4 tablespoons butter or margarine
> 2 tablespoons chopped onion
> 2 tablespoons vinegar
> 2 tablespoons finely chopped fresh parsley
> 1 teaspoon fresh tarragon
> 4 ripe tomatoes, diced
> 3 tablespoons oil

Cut fish into 4 servings. Season with salt and pepper. Mix egg and 2 tablespoons melted butter. Dip fish in egg mixture and then in bread crumbs. Let dry on wax paper or plastic wrap until ready to cook.

To make sauce, heat 2 tablespoons butter in a saucepan and cook onion until tender. Add vinegar, parsley, tarragon, and tomatoes. Cook about 5 minutes and keep hot.

Heat oil and remaining 2 tablespoons butter in a large skillet. Pan fry the breaded fillets, turning to brown both sides, about 6 to 8 minutes altogether. Serve fillets with tomato sauce. Makes 4 servings.

Fish Dinner for Two

When you are just two for dinner, here is a quick meal. With cole slaw and whole-wheat bread, and for dessert pound cake with sliced peaches, it's a take-it-easy dinner.

2 cups boiling water
1 cup uncooked medium noodles
2 tablespoons butter or margarine
1 green onion, chopped
½ to ¾ pound boneless fish fillets (ocean catfish, cod, haddock, or halibut)
1 ripe tomato, diced
1 tablespoon chopped fresh basil or 1 teaspoon dried, crushed
¼ cup chablis wine
1 tablespoon cornstarch

In a medium saucepan combine boiling water and noodles. Boil for 9 minutes. Drain well. Add butter and onion. Cut uncooked fish into cubes and fold into noodles with basil and tomatoes. Cook over medium heat 2 to 3 minutes, stirring. Mix wine and cornstarch and add to noodles. Cook and stir until mixture boils and is thickened. Makes 2 servings.

Fish with Broccoli and Cheese

Fish with Broccoli and Cheese is simple enough to make so that you can prepare it often. The colors of the broccoli and cheese added to the fish make it a pleasure to look at as well as good to eat. The dish may be prepared in advance except for baking. Refrigerate until ready to bake and add 5 minutes to baking time for the chilled dish.

8 medium spears fresh broccoli, trimmed and washed
2 pounds thin fish fillets
2 tablespoons lemon juice
2 tablespoons melted butter or margarine
4 slices American process cheese

Steam broccoli spears and arrange in 4 servings in buttered flat baking dish. Brush fish with lemon juice and butter and broil about 5 minutes. Divide broiled fillets into four servings and place over broccoli. Put one slice cheese on each serving of fish and bake at 450° F for about 5 minutes or until cheese melts. Makes 4 servings.

Fish Hash

This New England dish calls for a New England menu. Serve vinegar with the Fish Hash and complete the menu with buttered beets, Parker House rolls, and a fruit salad that can serve as a combination salad and dessert.

>3 slices bacon, diced
>1 cup chopped Spanish onion
>3 cups diced cooked potatoes
>1 teaspoon salt
>Freshly ground pepper to taste
>Dash Tabasco sauce
>2 cups cooked, flaked fish (cod, haddock, or other fish)

In a large skillet cook bacon until partially crisp. Add onion and continue cooking until onion is soft but not browned. Stir in potatoes, seasonings, and fish and spread evenly over the bottom of the skillet. Cook over medium heat until hash is brown and crusty. Use a spatula to turn and brown other side. Makes 4 to 6 servings.

Portuguese Style Fish and Chips

You'll find Portuguese fish and chips a tasty change from the "plain" version. Cole slaw is a standard addition to this combination.

    ½ cup cider vinegar
    1½ cups water
    1 clove garlic, crushed
    Dash ground cumin
    Dash dried oregano, crushed
    Salt and freshly ground pepper to taste
    2 pounds boneless fish fillets (cod, haddock, hake,
        ocean perch)
    ½ cup cornmeal (about)
    Shortening or oil for frying
    Frozen French fried potatoes for 4 servings, defrosted

Combine vinegar and water with seasonings in a glass or stainless steel bowl. Cut fish into serving size pieces and add to vinegar mixture. Let fish marinate in refrigerator for at least 2 hours, longer if possible. When ready to cook, remove fish from marinade and dip into cornmeal to cover. Let stand on wax paper while heating oil.

Heat shortening or oil at least 2 inches deep to 375° F. Fry potatoes to brown, about 3 minutes. Remove from oil with a slotted spoon and drain on paper towels. Keep hot in low (200° F) oven.

Let oil return to temperature and fry fish, turning to brown both sides, 5 minutes in all. Serve fish with French fried potatoes. Makes 4 servings.

Fish Fillets with Cheese Sauce

In this interesting recipe the fish is poached in beer and then served with a cheese sauce. Buttered noodles, cauliflower, carrot slaw, and rye bread will add to this tasty dish.

1 can (12 ounces) beer
2 pounds boneless fillets of ocean perch, hake, or cusk
4 cloves
1½ cups grated American process cheese
Freshly ground pepper to taste
2 teaspoons dry mustard
1 teaspoon paprika
2 teaspoons lemon juice
2 teaspoons Worcestershire sauce

Open beer an hour in advance and let stand so it will not foam when you pour it.

Roll fillets to make 4 servings, inserting a clove in each roll. Place in a pan that just holds fillets and pour over beer. Bring to a boil, reduce heat, poach fish 5 to 8 minutes until fish flakes easily with a fork. Remove from liquid and keep warm. Discard all but ¾ cup of the poaching beer. Add to it the cheese and all remaining ingredients. Cook, stirring, until cheese is melted and sauce is smooth. Serve over fish. Makes 4 servings.

Fish Souffle

The only difficult thing about making a souffle is being certain that the diners are at table when the souffle comes from the oven. My menu with a souffle is invariably hot buttered French bread and a large tossed green salad spiked with raw sliced mushrooms, tomato wedges, and a mixture of greens including fresh spinach. I like a strawberry sundae for dessert.

4 tablespoons butter or margarine
2 tablespoons finely chopped onion
4 tablespoons flour
1 cup fish stock
1 cup light cream
½ teaspoon salt
Dash Tabasco
2 tablespoons minced parsley
½ cup fine dry bread crumbs
2 cups cooked, flaked, boneless fish
4 eggs, separated

Heat butter and saute onions until clear. Do not brown. Stir in flour and let cook 1 to 2 minutes. Stir in fish broth and cream and cook and stir until mixture boils and is thickened. Remove from heat. Add salt, Tabasco, parsley, bread crumbs and fish flakes. Beat egg whites until very stiff. Beat egg yolks until thick and lemon colored and fold into fish mixture. Fold in egg whites. Pour into a 2-quart souffle dish. Bake at 325° F for about 1 hour. Serve at once. Makes 4 servings.

Fish Lover's Casserole

A slightly different casserole with which to tempt your family. Fill out the menu with fluffy mashed potatoes, buttered green beans, lettuce wedge with thousand-island dressing, and pears in red wine.

4 strips bacon, diced
1 small onion, chopped
1 clove garlic, chopped
½ green pepper, chopped
1 pound skinless and boneless hake or tautog fillets
1 can (16 ounces) cream style corn
½ teaspoon chili powder
1 cup crushed potato chips

Cook bacon until crisp. Remove from skillet and reserve. Saute onion, garlic, and green pepper in bacon fat until tender. Cut fish into bite-size pieces and combine all ingredients except chips, mixing lightly. Spoon into a well-buttered 6-cup casserole and top with crushed chips. Bake at 350° F for about 45 minutes or until bubbly. Makes 4 servings.

Baked Fillets with Puffy Cheese Sauce

Baked Fillets with Puffy Cheese Sauce look as good as they taste. Any boneless fish fillet can be used for this recipe. Put a dish of scalloped potatoes with onions and celery in the oven about 40 minutes before it is time to cook the fish. Then steam Chinese pea pods and heat bread at the last minute in the oven with the fish and potatoes. Have a small green salad. Sliced bananas with ice cream could be the dessert.

2 pounds boneless fish fillets
¾ cup mayonnaise
¼ cup grated American process cheese
2 egg yolks
2 tablespoons drained sweet pickle relish
½ teaspoon salt
2 egg whites

Divide fish into 4 portions. Place a single layer in a well-buttered baking pan. Combine remaining ingredients except egg whites. Beat egg whites until stiff and fold into mayonnaise mixture. Cover fish with mayonnaise mixture and bake at 350° F for 15 to 20 minutes or until topping is browned and fish flakes easily with a fork. Makes 4 servings.

Baked Fish Fillets Dennis Style

Baked Fish Fillets Dennis Style would take nicely to potato puffs, stewed tomatoes, celery sticks, and for dessert apple dumpling.

2 pounds boneless fish fillets (cod, haddock, or hake)
⅓ cup all-purpose flour
⅓ cup cornmeal
½ teaspoon onion salt
Freshly ground pepper to taste
4 tablespoons butter or margarine
⅓ cup grated Parmesan cheese

Cut fillets into 4 serving size pieces.

Mix flour, cornmeal, onion salt, and pepper in a flat pan. Melt butter in a flat baking dish. Dip fillets in flour mixture to cover both sides. Place in baking dish and turn to coat both sides with butter. Sprinkle with Parmesan cheese. Bake at 400° F for 25 minutes or until fish flakes. Makes 4 servings.

Fish with Chinese Sweet-and-Sour Sauce

What else but rice to serve with this recipe? Also steamed snow peas and sliced tomatoes, with fresh fruit for dessert. Chinese sweet-and-sour dishes are famous. Probably sweet-sour fish is not as popular here as it is in China, but it is a good combination.

2 pounds fish fillets (cod, haddock, or ocean catfish)
2 tablespoons butter or margarine
1 tablespoon lemon juice
Salt and freshly ground pepper to taste
1 tablespoon brown sugar
1½ teaspoons cornstarch
3 tablespoons water
3 tablespoons vinegar
3 tablespoons soy sauce
1 cup diagonally sliced celery
½ cup thinly sliced onions
½ cup canned pineapple chunks, drained

Cut fish into 4 serving size pieces and place in a buttered flat baking dish. Dot with butter and sprinkle with lemon juice. Season to taste with salt and pepper. Bake at 400° F for 25 minutes or until fish flakes easily.

Meanwhile make sauce. Combine brown sugar, cornstarch, water, vinegar, and soy sauce in a small saucepan. Cook and stir until mixture boils and is thickened. Add celery, onions, and pineapple and cook 2 minutes longer. Serve hot over cooked fish. Makes 4 servings.

Fish in Orange Sauce

Fish cooked with orange sauce may sound a little offbeat but it is an intriguing combination which you will like once you have tried it. Buttered new potatoes, peas with mushrooms, toasted hard rolls, lettuce with oil and vinegar, and cookies and tea for dessert will fill out the menu.

2 pounds fish fillets (cod, haddock, or ocean catfish)
5 tablespoons orange juice
1 teaspoon grated orange rind
3 tablespoons butter or margarine, melted
1 tablespoon lemon juice
Salt and freshly ground pepper to taste
Dash freshly ground nutmeg
Slivered toasted almonds

Place fish in a buttered 8 × 8-inch baking dish. Combine orange juice with rind, butter, lemon juice, salt, pepper, and nutmeg and pour over fish. Bake at 400° F for 25 minutes or until fish flakes easily with a fork. Garnish with toasted almonds. Makes 4 servings.

Easy Poached Fish with Mushroom Sauce

This quickly prepared fish dish for two is flavored with an envelope of soup mix. You can get everything else ready before the fish is cooked. Serve with rice or noodles to make the most of the sauce. A green vegetable such as steamed fresh spinach and a lettuce salad with your favorite dressing are good accompaniments. Baked pears will stand by for dessert.

    2 tablespoons butter or margarine
    1 envelope golden mushroom soup mix
    1 tablespoon chopped fresh parsley
    ¾ cup water
    1 pound boneless fish fillets (cod, haddock, ocean cat-
        fish, hake, or tautog)

In medium skillet, melt butter. Blend soup mix and parsley with water and stir into butter. Add fish fillets and simmer 10 minutes or until fish flakes easily with a fork. Serve sauce with fish. Makes 2 servings.

Fish and Macaroni Casserole

Canned soups are commonly used in recipes, in fact some varieties are used more in cooking than as soup. But the dry soup mixes have a real place in recipes too. They are easy to store, add great flavor, and save kitchen work. This casserole is a good example of dry soup cookery. With it serve wax beans, apple cole slaw, and perhaps frozen eclairs for dessert.

    1 envelope golden mushroom soup mix
    1½ cups milk
    ½ pound elbow macaroni, cooked and drained
    2 cups cooked and flaked boneless fish (tautog, dogfish,
        bluefish)
    2 tablespoons finely chopped parsley
    2 tablespoons finely chopped pimiento
    ½ cup buttered bread crumbs

In a buttered 2-quart casserole blend soup mix with milk. Stir in macaroni, fish flakes, parsley, and pimiento. Top with bread crumbs. Bake at 350° F for 35 minutes or until bubbly. Makes 4 servings.

Fish Baked with Onion Rings

Mashed potato cakes, yellow summer squash sauteed with chopped parsley, whole-wheat bread, and fruit gelatin for dessert will show off the Fish Baked with Onion Rings.

1½ to 2 pounds skinned fillets of hake, tautog, or cusk
1 cup dairy sour cream (or yogurt)
½ teaspoon salt
¼ teaspoon garlic powder
Paprika
1 can (2.8 ounces) French fried onion rings

Place fillets in a buttered flat baking dish. Mix sour cream with salt and garlic powder. (Substitute plain yogurt for sour cream for a lower-calorie dish.) Spread over fillets and sprinkle with paprika. Top with onion rings. Bake at 400° F about 30 minutes or until fish flakes easily with a fork. Cover top lightly with foil if onion rings start to become too brown. Makes 4 servings.

Cornmeal Fried Fish with Hush Puppies

Now and then it is fun to prepare a fish dish that is off the New England beat. Cornmeal Fried Fish with Hush Puppies, a traditional Southern combination, falls into that category. I remember eating it at a dinner in New York City. The husband of the couple who had invited us was from the South. The wife was from New England. She had "learned" to make Hush Puppies, but not very well. My husband, a New Englander, had a few words for them when we got home. Properly made, however, they are delicious.

Small whole fish, cleaned and heads removed, or boneless fish fillets (cod, haddock, or scrod)
Undiluted evaporated milk
Yellow cornmeal
Fat for frying

If you are using fillets, cut them in serving pieces. Dip fish first in evaporated milk, then in cornmeal.

Fry in fairly hot fat (375° F) about 2 inches deep, turning to brown both sides. A fish or piece of fish to serve one person should be cooked in about 5 minutes. Keep hot in a 200° F oven while frying Hush Puppies to be served with fried fish.

Hush Puppies

1½ cups yellow cornmeal
½ cup all-purpose flour
2 teaspoons baking powder
½ teaspoon salt
1 egg
2 tablespoons chopped onion
¾ cup milk
Fat for frying

Mix cornmeal with flour, baking powder, and salt in a bowl. Add egg, onion, and milk and stir to blend. Fry in fairly hot fat (375° F) about 2 inches deep by dropping tablespoons of the batter into fat. Turn to brown both sides. Hush puppies will be cooked in 4 to 5 minutes. Makes about 20.

Fish "Sausage"

Serve Fish "Sausage" with scrambled eggs and toasted English muffins for a hearty breakfast. Or serve it as an entree with hashed brown potatoes, dill pickles, rye bread, and a mixed vegetable salad. Use boneless, skinless scraps of any fish for this recipe. If the fish is partially frozen in the freezer it is easier to remove the skin.

2 pounds boneless, skinless scraps of fish
20 single saltines
1 medium onion
½ teaspoon salt
Freshly ground pepper to taste
1 teaspoon Bell's poultry seasoning
¼ teaspoon celery salt
¼ teaspoon garlic powder
2 teaspoons Dijon style mustard
1 tablespoon lemon juice

In a food processor, using steel blade, process fish about one-half pound at a time until finely ground. Put into a bowl as processed. When fish is finished, process crackers and onion until finely ground. Mix with fish and seasonings. Let fish stand in refrigerator to blend flavors. (Can be prepared and refrigerated overnight if one wishes.) Shape into patties and fry in bacon fat or butter. Makes 8 patties.

· SHELL FISH ·

Steamed Clams

Steamed clams make a fine first or main course. (Except at a clambake or picnic, they are a little messy for an hors d'oeuvre.) Knowing the appetite of the eaters is important. I can eat 2 dozen with no problem. But whether you cook 6 or 60, the directions are the same.

Wash, scrub and rinse steamer clams thoroughly in cold water. Place in a pan large enough to hold the clams, and add ½ to 1 cup water depending on the number of steamers. Cover and bring to a boil. Simmer about 5 minutes or until shells begin to open.

Remove clams from pan with fork or slotted spoon and divide among shallow soup dishes. Strain broth through cheesecloth and pour into cups, 1 for each person. Have melted butter for dipping and bone plates on which to put the empty shells.

To eat, pull off the black skin covering the neck and discard on the bone plate. Dip clam in broth and then in butter. Eat and enjoy. Any broth left in cup should be drunk.

You will need plenty of paper napkins.

White Clam Sauce

White clam sauce is so easy to make and so good. Here is my favorite way to serve it. Add a tossed green salad and hot bread to this combination.

> 4 tablespoons butter or margarine
> 1 or 2 cloves garlic, minced
> 1 tablespoon flour
> 2 cups chopped raw clams and their juice*
> 4 tablespoons chopped fresh parsley
> Salt and freshly ground pepper to taste
> 1 pound thin spaghetti or linguine, cooked, drained,
>   and tossed with additional butter

Heat butter in skillet. Add garlic and cook for several minutes, but do not brown. Stir in flour and cook until mixture bubbles. Stir in clam juice and parsley and season with salt and pepper. Cook and stir over low heat for 5 minutes. Stir in clams and heat through. Serve with hot spaghetti. Makes 4 servings.

Red Clam Sauce

A variation is Red Clam Sauce: Add 4 tablespoons tomato paste with the clam juice, stirring to blend. Proceed with the rest of the recipe as directed.

*If you are using defrosted frozen clams and have frozen the clams and juice separately, use about ½ cup juice with 2 cups raw clams.

Quick Clam Pancakes

Clam pancakes are an old Cape custom. Some people even like to eat them with real maple syrup or honey. Personally, I like them slathered with butter. For a breakfast menu, try a half of grapefruit to start, lots of clam pancakes, and with doughnuts and coffee to finish off.

> 2 cups buttermilk baking mix
> 2 eggs
> 1 cup milk *or* half milk and half clam juice
> 1 cup drained raw chopped clams

Blend baking mix with eggs and liquid. Beat with a hand beater until smooth. Fold in clams.

Pour about ¼ cup batter on hot greased griddle. Cook until dry around the edges. Turn and cook until golden brown. Makes about 15 pancakes.

Flounder Fillets with Clam Stuffing

In the spring and fall the fishermen and women start fishing for flounder off the Bass River Bridge. That is one place where no license is required, and with luck you can have a mess of delicious fish. In this recipe flounders are filleted to remove bones and skin and combined with the clam diggers' bounty of clams. Of course you can always buy flounder and clams at your favorite fish market.

1 medium onion, finely chopped
½ cup finely chopped celery
2 tablespoons butter or margarine
¼ cup clam juice
½ cup chopped fresh clams
1½ cups soft whole-wheat bread crumbs
1 egg, lightly beaten
8 equal size flounder fillets
2 tablespoons fresh lemon juice
3 tablespoons butter or margarine, melted
¼ cup chopped fresh parsley

Saute onion and celery in 2 tablespoons butter in a medium skillet until soft but not browned. Mix in clam juice, clams, bread crumbs, and egg until well blended. Set stuffing aside.

Place 4 fillets, skin side down, in a well-buttered baking dish. Divide stuffing equally among fillets, spreading to edges. Place remaining fillets skin side up on top of stuffing. Sprinkle with lemon juice and melted butter. Bake at 400° F for 25 to 30 minutes or until fish flakes. Serve sprinkled with chopped parsley. Makes 4 servings.

Scalloped Clams

Scalloped Clams are a tasty solution if your freezer is overloaded with chopped clams from clamming. Scalloped clams would taste good with steamed sliced celery, lightly sauteed cherry tomatoes, and apple cobbler.

2 cups soft whole-wheat bread crumbs
2 cups chopped clams
1 cup clam juice
½ cup melted butter or margarine

In a buttered 4-cup casserole, alternately layer crumbs and clams, beginning and ending with crumbs. Mix clam juice and butter and pour over casserole. Bake at 375° F for about 35 minutes. Makes 2 to 4 servings, depending on appetites.

The Clambake

Visitors to the Cape are always looking for professional clambakes to attend. A clambake is a setting where luscious seafood is at its best. Get there early enough to watch the tarpaulin come off the cooking food. The bouquet of aromas is ambrosial.

If you can't manage a professional clambake, it is possible to have your own. You'll need a wash boiler or a *large* enamel pot, seaweed, and cheesecloth. For 6 people this is the food list.

At least 4 dozen steamer clams
6 potatoes, skin on, scrubbed
6 ears of corn, unhusked
6 whole medium onions
6 frankfurters or sausages
6 live lobsters, about 1 pound each
Melted butter
Cole slaw (if desired)
Hot buttered crusty bread
Clam juice (if desired)
Watermelon

Discard all broken and dead clams. (Dead clams float in the water when you are washing them.) The lobsters should be of the same size, about 1 pound each, and have at least one wiggling flipper.

Now, fill the bottom of the boiler or pot with 6 inches of wet seaweed. Divide the steamers among 6 pieces of cheesecloth and tie corners so you can pick them up. Place on seaweed. Remove silk and all but one or two layers of husk from corn. Place corn, potatoes, onions, and frankfurters or sausage over the clams in that order. Top off with the lobsters. Put a layer of cheesecloth over the lobsters and cover with another 6 inches of wet seaweed. Cover closely and place boiler or pot over high heat. When steaming begins, reduce heat to moderate and cook for one hour and 15 minutes. Serve with the melted butter, cole slaw, and bread.

While waiting for bake to cook, you might serve clam juice, either canned or left from quahogs. Watermelon wedges are a must for dessert.

Clam Pie

There are many versions of clam pie. This one, a little more elaborate than some, is a deliciously flavored way to serve up clams.

3 dozen hard-shelled clams (about 3½ cups chopped clams)
½ cup water
¼ cup butter or margarine
½ cup sliced fresh mushrooms
2 tablespoons minced onion
¼ cup all-purpose flour
1 teaspoon prepared hot mustard
Freshly ground pepper to taste
1 cup reserved clam juice
1 cup half-and-half
1 tablespoon fresh lemon juice
3 tablespoons chopped fresh parsley
2 tablespoons chopped pimiento (optional)
Pastry for 1 9-inch pie crust

Scrub and rinse clams well. Combine with water in a large pan and bring to a boil. Simmer just until clams open, 4 to 5 minutes. Drain liquid from pan into another container and reserve. When clams are cool enough, remove from shells and chop.

Melt butter in a skillet and saute mushrooms and onion until tender. Add flour, mustard, and pepper and cook and stir 2 minutes. Gradually add clam juice and half-and-half and cook and stir until mixture boils and is thickened. Combine with lemon juice, parsley, pimiento, and clams. Spoon into a buttered deep 9-inch pie plate or casserole (about 2 inches deep). Roll out crust and cut to fit container. Place on container and crimp edges to secure to rim of container. Cut slits in top to allow steam to escape. Bake at 375° F for 25 to 30 minutes or until pastry is browned and filling bubbles through slits. Makes one 9-inch pie.

Cape Cod Clam Pie

A friend who is a descendant of native Cape Codders (she had the misfortune to be born off Cape) gave me this recipe for Clam Pie. It is more typical of a Cape Cod clam pie than the preceding recipe and is a delicious way to serve clams. It is a fond memory of one of our first parties here on the Cape. I insisted that among the foods on the buffet should be clam pie. Against my husband's will, it was. It turned out to more popular than the usual roast beef and ham.

>   10 medium sea clams or 2 pints quahogs, cleaned
>   3 ounces salt pork, diced
>   ½ cup chopped onions
>   1 cup common cracker crumbs*
>   ½ pint light cream
>   Pastry for 2-crust 9-inch pie

Chop or grind clams.

Fry salt pork until crisp. Add the onions and clams and cook 2 to 3 minutes. Stir in crumbs and cream. Remove from heat.

Line a 9-inch pie plate with half the pastry and fill with clam mixture. Roll out remaining pastry and cover filling with rolled pastry. Press bottom and top edges together and decorate edge with fork or fingers. Cut several slits in top to allow steam to escape. Bake pie at 425° F for 30 to 40 minutes, until pastry browns lightly and filling bubbles. If pie crust gets too brown on rim, cover with aluminum foil. Serve hot or cold.

>   *Common crackers are what we call today soda crackers. Use unsalted soda crackers.

Poor Man's Oysters

The friend who gave me this recipe for eggplant and clams calls it "Poor Man's Oysters" since the baked combination tastes so much like oysters. After preparing it I agree with her. Serve with julienned cooked carrots, steamed snow peas, fresh cubed pineapple.

1 medium eggplant (about 1 pound)
Boiling salted water
¾ cup dry bread crumbs
1 cup drained, minced raw clams
Freshly ground pepper to taste
¼ teaspoon garlic salt
3 tablespoons grated Parmesan cheese
3 tablespoons melted butter or margarine
½ cup clam juice
¼ cup buttered dry bread crumbs
2 tablespoons grated Parmesan cheese

Peel eggplant and cut into 1-inch squares. There should be about 5 cups. Cover with boiling water with a little salt added and cook until tender, about 10 minutes. Drain. Mix ¾ cup bread crumbs, clams, pepper, garlic salt, 3 tablespoons grated Parmesan cheese, melted butter, and clam juice. Combine with drained eggplant.

Spoon into a buttered 4-cup baking dish. Sprinkled with buttered bread crumbs and 2 tablespoons grated Parmesan cheese. Bake at 350° F for 35 to 40 minutes. Makes 4 servings.

Herbed Clam Sauce for Spaghetti

A crisp hot French bread and a tossed salad would make this a full meal.

2 tablespoons finely chopped onion
1 tablespoon butter or margarine
½ cup dry white wine
¾ cup evaporated milk
½ cup clam juice
1 tablespoon cornstarch
3 tablespoons finely chopped chives
1 teaspoon finely chopped fresh tarragon or ⅓ teaspoon
  dried, crushed
3 tablespoons finely chopped fresh basil or 1 tablespoon
  dried, crushed
¾ to 1 cup chopped fresh clams
Salt and freshly ground pepper to taste
1 pound thin spaghetti, cooked and drained

Saute onion in butter until soft but not browned. Add wine and reduce over moderate heat until about 2 tablespoons remain. Add evaporated milk. Blend clam juice and cornstarch and add to evaporated milk mixture. Bring to a boil and let simmer several minutes, stirring until thickened. Stir in herbs and clams, season with salt and pepper as needed, and bring just to boiling point. Let stand, covered, over very low heat for about 5 minutes. Serve over spaghetti. Makes 4 servings.

Boiled or Steamed Lobster

All visitors to Cape Cod must have lobster before they leave, whether their stay is for the weekend or the summer. If you have facilities where it can be eaten, all the fish markets will steam the lobster for you. At the height of the season get your order in early, as most markets do a land office business during July and August. Certain pieces of equipment make easier eating of whole lobster, boiled or baked. An old-fashioned nutcracker to use in cracking the claws is one. I also have lobster forks which are long and thin with two prongs at the working end to dig the lobster out of the small legs and joints. You can eat a lobster without these aids, but they do make it easier.

All of a lobster (excepting the bony shell, of course) is edible except for the small craw in the head of the lobster and the dark vein running down the back of the body meat. (Even the bony shell is used in lobster stock.)

The green mass is the liver or tomalley. The red or brown coral, if found, is the female lobster's undeveloped spawn (eggs). Both are excellent eating.

Place the live lobster in a kettle which contains about 2 inches of boiling salted water. (Some Cape Codders insist that lobster cannot be properly boiled in anything but ocean water. If it is available, fine. Otherwise use tap water and add a bit of salt.) Cover kettle immediately. When water returns to a boil cook lobster according to this schedule.

12 minutes	1-pound lobster
20 minutes	1¼-pound lobster
25 minutes	1½-pound lobster
30 minutes	2- to 3-pound lobster

Baked or Broiled Stuffed Lobster

Personally, I have never been an advocate of broiled lobster because it always seems to me that the claw meat becomes overcooked and tough when cooked in a broiler. Here is a recipe which may be used baked or broiled, but I recommend the former.

1½ cups cracker crumbs (I use Ritz crackers)
1 teaspoon Worcestershire sauce
½ cup melted butter or margarine
Tomalley
4 lobsters, 1¼ to 1½ pounds each
Wet lettuce leaves to cover (optional)
Additional melted butter for dipping

If you haven't yet worked yourself up to splitting a live lobster, the fish market will do it for you. But one should not split a lobster until about an hour before the cooking, and it is not always convenient to go to the fish market in the summer traffic in the last hour before a meal. So I have learned how to split a lobster. (You'd be surprised how many market clerks are unknowledgeable about it.) I'll give you directions at the end of this recipe.

A market split lobster will have the craw and dark vein removed.

Mix cracker crumbs, Worcestershire sauce, butter, and tomalley until well blended. Lay split lobsters shell side down on a large pan and fill cavity of each with stuffing. I have never found it necessary to cover stuffing with wet lettuce leaves but some experts recommend that.

Baking: Prepare lobsters as directed (the lettuce leaves may be omitted) and bake at 400° F for 25 minutes. Serve with additional melted butter.

Broiling: Place stuffed lobsters on broiler pan 8 to 10 inches from heating unit and broil 25 to 30 minutes. Remove lettuce leaves (if used) and serve with additional melted butter.

Makes 4 servings.

How to Split a Live Lobster

Start with a sharp knife. A boning size knife with a good point is ideal. Lay the lobster on its back on a board or other surface that cannot be injured. Hold claws firmly, make a deep incision in the body in between where the claws are attached, and cut right down through the tail. Do not cut the lobster completely in two, but split it enough so that you can bend it open for stuffing. (This takes a little practice.) The craw is right at the head of the lobster and should be removed. The black intestinal vein should also be removed. Take out the tomalley to use in the stuffing, and the coral, if any. (I keep saying "if any" because in all the lobsters I have cooked, I've only found coral once.) Rinse the lobster under running water and stuff to cook.

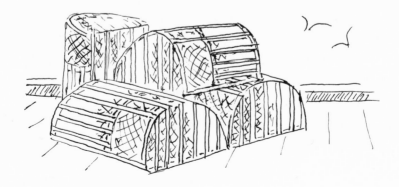

Lobster Newburg

A classic dish that is always popular. Served with buttered fresh green beans, Boston lettuce with oil and vinegar, and orange sherbet for dessert, it makes a delightful special lunch or supper.

1 cooked lobster, about 2 pounds
¼ cup butter
¼ cup all-purpose flour
2 cups half-and-half
½ cup dry sherry
2 egg yolks, beaten
Salt and freshly ground pepper to taste
4 baked puff pastry shells

Remove meat from lobster and cut into medium dice. Saute in butter for several minutes. Stir in flour and half-and-half and bring to a boil. Add sherry and reheat. Add about 1 cup of hot mixture to egg yolks, mixing well. Combine with rest of lobster mixture, stirring to blend. Hold over low heat for 2 to 3 minutes but do not boil. Add salt and pepper to taste. Serve in puff pastry shells. Makes 4 servings.

Mussels in Tomato Sauce

Steamed zucchini, French bread, and greens with Italian dressing are good partners for Mussels in Tomato Sauce. Have pound cake and hot tea for dessert.

2 quarts mussels
¼ cup dry white wine
1 medium onion, chopped
1 clove garlic, chopped
¼ cup olive oil
1 stalk celery, chopped
½ green pepper, seeded and chopped
1 can (8 ounces) tomato sauce
⅔ cup mussel broth
¼ cup chopped fresh parsley
1 tablespoon chopped fresh basil or 1 teaspoon dried, crushed
Hot cooked rice or macaroni

Clean and debeard mussels. Steam in wine until just opened, 3 to 4 minutes. Discard any that do not open. Cool and shuck mussels. Reserve mussels. Discard shells. Strain broth and measure ⅔ cup.

Saute onion and garlic in olive oil until tender but not browned. Add remaining ingredients except mussels and rice and simmer slowly, covered, for about 30 minutes. Add mussels and reheat. Serve with rice or macaroni. Makes 4 servings.

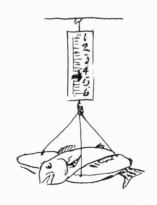

Bass with Mussels

Serve this elegant dish with steamed rice, spinach, and fresh pear salad.

1 pound mussels
¼ pound fresh mushrooms
2 green onions, chopped
2 tablespoons lemon juice
¼ cup dry white wine
2 pounds boneless fillets of black bass, tilefish, or cod
2 tablespoons butter or margarine, melted
1 tablespoon cornstarch
2 tablespoons water

Clean and debeard mussels. Steam in ½ cup water until shells open. Discard any that do not open. When cool enough to handle, remove mussels from shell. Cut each into 2 or 3 pieces and place in a bowl. Clean mushrooms and chop. Add mushrooms, onions, lemon juice, and wine to mussels.

Butter well a flat baking dish and scatter mussel mixture on bottom of dish. Place fillets, skin side up, on top of mussel mixture. Spread with melted butter. Bake at 400° F for about 30 minutes or until fish flakes easily. To serve, use a spatula and turn fillets skin side down on warmed platter or individual dinner plates. Mix cornstarch and water and add to mussels and pan juices. Bring quickly to a boil to thicken. Spoon over fish. Makes 4 servings.

Creamed Mussels

These creamed mussels can be heated in one larger casserole if it is not convenient to use individual dishes. Serve with rice amandine, Frenched green beans, romaine with orange sections and onion rings, and butter pecan ice cream.

2 quarts mussels
1 onion, chopped
1 clove garlic, cut in half
2 sprigs parsley
½ cup dry white wine
4 tablespoons butter or margarine
3 tablespoons flour
½ cup broth from mussels
1 cup milk
Salt and freshly ground pepper to taste
Freshly ground nutmeg to taste
Grated Parmesan or Romano cheese

Clean and debeard mussels. Combine onion, garlic, parsley, and wine and simmer, covered, 15 minutes. Add mussels and steam until just opened, 3 to 4 minutes. Discard any that do not open. Strain broth and measure ½ cup. Cool mussels and shuck. Reserve mussels. Discard shells.

Melt butter in a medium saucepan. Add flour and cook 2 minutes. Stir in mussel broth, gradually add milk, and cook and stir until mixture boils and is thickened. Season to taste with salt, pepper, and nutmeg. Add mussels and reheat. Divide among 4 individual casseroles and sprinkle lightly with Parmesan or Romano cheese. Run under broiler for several minutes until lightly browned. Makes 4 servings.

Deviled Mussels

Deviled Mussels would make a delicious first course or could serve as a main course. Baked stuffed potatoes, zucchini sauteed with tomatoes, hot French bread, a tossed salad, and fresh pears for dessert would round out a dandy meal.

24 large mussels
¼ cup water
6 tablespoons butter or margarine
3 tablespoons minced onion
1 clove garlic, minced
1 tablespoon minced parsley
¼ cup stale beer
4 slices bacon, crisply cooked and crumbled
4 tablespoons (or more) dry bread crumbs

Clean and debeard mussels. Steam in ¼ cup water, covered, just until mussels open, about 2 minutes. Discard 1 shell from each mussel and reserve remaining shell. Remove mussels and chop in food processor with steel blade or in a blender.

Cream together butter, onion, garlic, and parsley. Blend in beer, then mix in mussels and bacon.

Fill mussel shells with mixture and sprinkle with bread crumbs. Place on a baking sheet and bake at 375° F for 10 minutes. Serves 6 as a first course or 4 as a main course.

Curried Mussels

If three teaspoons curry powder sounds a little heavy to you, cut it back to two. Besides rice, serve cranberry relish, buttered broccoli, sliced tomatoes, and for dessert lemon or orange sherbet.

2 quarts mussels
¼ cup dry white wine
5 tablespoons butter or margarine
¼ cup chopped green onions
1 clove garlic, chopped
1 small apple, peeled, cored, and diced
3 teaspoons curry powder
2 tablespoons flour
1 cup mussel broth
½ cup cream
Salt and freshly ground pepper to taste
2 to 3 cups hot cooked rice

Clean and debeard mussels. Steam mussels in wine until just opened, 3 to 4 minutes. Cool and shuck mussels. Remove mussels and discard shells. Strain broth and measure 1 cup.

Heat butter in a saucepan and saute onions, garlic, and apple until soft but not browned. Add curry powder and flour and mix well. Stir in mussel broth and cream and cook and stir until mixture boils and is thickened. Season to taste with salt and pepper. Add mussels and simmer until mussels are heated. Serve over hot cooked rice. Makes 4 servings.

Scalloped Oysters

In some families scalloped oysters are traditional Christmas Eve fare because they are easy to prepare and a light meal before the next day's festivities. If the scalloped oysters are being served as a light supper, plan the rest of the menu with restraint. Serve hot rolls and a dish of pickles with the oysters and for dessert a big bowl of mixed fresh fruit.

⅔ cup melted butter
3 cups soft white bread crumbs
½ teaspoon salt (optional)
¼ teaspoon ground mace
1½ pints oysters
¼ cup oyster liquor
¼ cup light cream

Toss butter, bread crumbs, salt, and mace together lightly. Butter well a flat 1-quart casserole. Put in half the crumbs. Pick out any pieces of shell from oysters and drain well, reserving liquor. Layer oysters over crumbs. Top with remaining crumbs. Mix oyster liquor and cream and pour over casserole. Bake at 375° F for 30 minutes. Makes 4 servings.

Oyster Pie

Oyster pie makes a lovely dish during the holidays. Appropriate companions are cranberry sauce, a winter vegetable such as baked squash, and for dessert a lemon or orange sherbet.

1 pint oysters
Oyster liquor
Milk
3 tablespoons butter or margarine
1 cup thinly sliced celery
2 teaspoons grated onion
2 tablespoons flour
3 tablespoons chopped fresh parsley
Pinch dried thyme
¼ teaspoon salt
¼ teaspoon freshly grated nutmeg
Freshly ground pepper to taste
Biscuit topping (below)

Drain oysters, reserving liquor, and remove any bits of shell. Add enough milk to oyster liquor to make 1 cup.

Heat butter and cook celery and onion over low heat about 5 minutes. Blend in flour. Stir in oyster liquid and milk and cook and stir until thickened. Add parsley, seasonings, and oysters. Spoon into a buttered 5 cup casserole. Top with biscuit topping. Bake at 400° F for 20 to 25 minutes or until browned. Makes 4 servings.

Biscuit Topping

Mix together 1 cup all-purpose flour, 1 teaspoon baking powder, and ½ teaspoon salt. Cut in ¼ cup shortening until blended. Stir in 1 lightly beaten small egg and enough milk to make a soft dough. Roll out about ½ inch thick on a floured board. Cut into 2-inch biscuits and place on oyster mixture.

* * *

Scallops are most plentiful in the fall and early winter. The whole scallop is edible, but in this country we eat only the muscle. Shucked scallops can be frozen at 0° F and will keep 6 months.

Bay scallops are found in shallow waters, ocean scallops in deeper ocean waters. Scallops are never sold in the shell. This mollusk cannot close its shell tightly. It dries out and dies when taken from the water. The scallop should be shucked very quickly after digging.

To shuck scallops, scrub shells well. Place them on a flat pan in a warm (200° F) oven. When shell rises slightly, use a knife to cut carefully the muscle where it is attached to the top shell. Then cut the muscle away from the bottom shell. Discard the membrane and guts around the muscle.

Unless one lives in an area where scallops can be harvested by residential permit, they are generally sold in fish markets by the pound. Bay scallops are tiny with a sweet flavor. Ocean scallops, the larger size, are not considered quite the delicacy bays are. Recently we have also been getting calico scallops from Florida. Anyone connected with local scalloping and retailing thinks the calico scallops are much inferior. However, they are considerably less expensive and have become a popular substitute. They should always be labeled "calico" so that if one has strong feelings toward bay or ocean scallops they will know if they are buying calicos.

To me, scallops' delicate flavor is best when they are treated simply (broiled or sauteed). But many recipes are more elaborate. Here is a sampling.

Broiled Scallops

Cook quickly and serve at once while hot. Broiled scallops can be served on toast, if desired, to soak up the good buttery juice. Steam small potatoes and cubed carrots to serve with scallops. Cranberry sauce and pear salad on crisp lettuce could be a salad-dessert combination with the scallop meal.

1 pound bay or ocean scallops
Melted butter or margarine
Fresh lemon juice
Paprika
Lemon wedges
Toast points (if desired)

Roll scallops in melted butter and sprinkle with lemon juice in the broiler pan or other pan with low sides. Sprinkle with paprika. Broil about 4 inches from source of heat, shaking pan once or twice, not longer than 3 minutes for bay scallops or 5 minutes for ocean. Serve at once on toast points with juice from pan and lemon wedges. Makes 4 servings.

Sauteed Scallops

Ocean scallops can be cut in halves or quarters to cook more quickly if one wishes.

3 tablespoons butter or margarine
1 pound bay or ocean scallops
2 tablespoons fresh lemon juice
4 tablespoons dried bread crumbs

Heat butter in a skillet large enough to hold scallops. Add scallops and stir over heat for 4 to 5 minutes until scallops are no longer opaque. Sprinkle with lemon juice and bread crumbs and serve at once. Makes 4 servings.

Baked Scallops

Bay scallops, the tiny gems of flavor that are such a treat, are delicious sauteed or broiled. Ocean scallops would fit better into this recipe for baked.

2 pounds ocean scallops
Hot water
2 tablespoons cider vinegar
Fine dry bread crumbs
2 eggs
2 tablespoons water
4 slices bacon, diced

Pick out any pieces of shell that might be in scallops and put scallops in bowl and rinse. Pour boiling water over scallops and add vinegar. Let stand 2 to 3 minutes. Drain and dry. Roll scallops in crumbs, then in eggs beaten with water and again in crumbs. Place close together in a buttered flat casserole. Scatter bacon over scallops. Bake at 400° F for 25 minutes. Makes 6 servings.

Scallops en Casserole

If you have scallop-shaped individual shells or casseroles, use them for this recipe. Fresh or frozen peas cooked with sliced water chestnuts, steamed acorn squash, peach and cottage cheese salad on lettuce, and apple sauce with cookies could complete the menu.

4 tablespoons butter or margarine
½ pound fresh mushrooms, sliced
1 green onion, chopped
2 tablespoons flour
1 cup dry white wine
1 tablespoon lemon juice
½ teaspoon salt
Freshly ground pepper to taste
1½ pounds bay or ocean scallops
2 tablespoons chopped fresh parsley
1 cup buttered crumbs

Heat butter in skillet and saute mushrooms and onions until tender. Stir in flour and cook 2 minutes. Add wine and cook and stir until mixture boils and is thickened. Add lemon juice, salt, and pepper. Stir in scallops (if ocean scallops are used, cut in half) and parsley. Spoon into a buttered shallow casserole or individual casseroles and sprinkle with crumbs. Bake at 400° F for 25 minutes. Makes 6 servings.

Netta's Scallop Casserole

This easy scallop casserole would be good with noodles or rice, steamed broccoli, tossed mixed salad with tomato wedges, and Irish coffee for dessert.

½ pound mushrooms, sliced
3 tablespoons butter or margarine
2 tablespoons flour
1 cup light cream
1 to 3 tablespoons dry vermouth
Salt and freshly ground pepper to taste
1 pound bay or ocean scallops
1 cup buttered crumbs

Pan fry mushrooms in butter until golden brown. Stir in flour and cream and bring to a boil, stirring, until thickened. Stir in vermouth to taste along with salt and pepper. Remove any pieces of shell from scallops and wash and drain well. Cut ocean scallops, if used, in half. Add scallops to sauce and spoon into a buttered 6-cup shallow casserole. Sprinkle top with crumbs. Cover and bake at 350° F for 30 minutes. Makes 4 servings.

Scallops with Garlic

Scallops should be cooked very quickly. These with a touch of garlic are easy to do and have a Mediterranean flavor. Buttered pasta, green beans, apple-celery salad, and a dessert of ice cream add to the enjoyment of the meal.

> 1½ pounds bay or ocean scallops
> Flour seasoned with salt, pepper, and paprika
> 6 tablespoons olive oil
> 1 clove garlic, minced
> Salt and freshly ground pepper to taste
> ½ cup chopped fresh parsley
> Toast points

If ocean scallops are used, cut in half. Dredge scallops in flour mixture. Heat oil in large skillet. Add scallops and garlic and cook quickly, about 4 to 5 minutes, stirring so scallops cook evenly. Add salt, pepper, and parsley. Serve on toast points. Makes 4 servings.

* * *

Quick Shrimp and Rice

This quickly prepared shrimp dish will be very popular. Add steamed Chinese pea pods and a wedge of lettuce with oil and vinegar dressing to the shrimp and rice. Mixed fresh fruit over vanilla ice cream is the dessert choice.

> 1 pound medium shrimp (about 24)
> ¼ cup olive oil
> 4 green onions, chopped
> 1 cup diced fresh tomatoes
> 1 cup sliced fresh mushrooms
> ½ cup grated Parmesan cheese
> ¼ cup dry white wine
> ¼ cup chopped fresh parsley
> 3 cups hot cooked rice

Shell, devein, and wash shrimp. Dry well. Heat olive oil in skillet. Add shrimp and cook and stir until shrimp turns pink. Add onions, tomatoes, and mushrooms and stir to blend with shrimp. Stir in cheese and wine and cook and stir until hot. Stir in parsley. Serve at once over hot rice. Makes 4 servings.

Shrimp Vegetable Squares

Steamed brown rice, lightly sauteed cherry tomatoes, and whole-wheat bread help make the Shrimp Squares a good main course. Fresh fruit is suggested for dessert.

> ½ pound cooked, peeled shrimp
> 1 package (10 ounces) frozen chopped spinach,
>   defrosted
> 1 cup grated sharp Cheddar cheese
> ½ cup finely chopped green onions
> 1 cup half-and-half
> 1 cup fish stock
> 2 eggs
> ½ teaspoon crushed dried basil or 1½ teaspoons fresh

Devein shrimp and cut in small dice. Drain spinach well, pressing against strainer or colander. Combine shrimp and spinach with remaining ingredients, mixing well. Spoon into a buttered casserole 8 or 9 inches square. Bake at 325° F for 30 minutes or until firm. Cut into squares to serve. Makes 4 servings.

Stuffed Shrimp

A rare treat. Serve with fresh asparagus, baked potatoes, and sliced garden tomatoes.

> 1 pound large (16 count) green shrimp in shell
> ¾ cup round butter cracker crumbs
> ¼ cup melted butter
> ¾ cup chopped fresh clams
> 1 clove garlic, finely minced
> 3 tablespoons chopped parsley
> Freshly ground pepper to taste
> ½ cup dry vermouth

Remove shells from shrimp, leaving tail shell on. Cut along sand vein side about halfway through the shrimp and wash well to remove sand vein. Dry.

Mix together crumbs, butter, clams, garlic, parsley, and pepper until well blended. If stuffing needs a little binding, add a few drops of vermouth. Stuff shrimp where cut and arrange in a flat, well-buttered baking dish in one layer. Bake at 350° F for 15 minutes or until shrimp turns pink. Baste several times with vermouth. Makes 4 servings.

Fried Shrimp in Batter

Fried shrimp is a favorite always. French fried potatoes make a good partner. They are quickly heated in the hot fat before the shrimp is cooked and kept hot in a 200° F oven.

1½ pounds medium green shrimp
¾ cup all-purpose flour
½ cup stale beer
1 tablespoon oil
1 egg
Shortening or oil for frying

Shell shrimp, leaving on tails, and remove sand vein.

Combine flour, beer, and oil. Separate egg yolk and white. Stir egg yolk into flour mixture. Beat egg white until stiff and fold into batter.

Heat shortening to 375° F (have at least 2 inches of hot fat or oil). Dip shrimp in batter and fry about 4 minutes, turning if necessary to brown both sides. Remove shrimp from hot fat with fork or slotted spoon. Drain on paper towels. Serve at once with catsup or Dijon style mustard. Makes 4 servings.

Fried Calamari (Squid) Rings

Once you've tried fried calamari rings you will find them at least equal to fried clams. Some people think they are better.

Keep the calamari rings hot in a 200° F oven and quickly brown frozen French fries in the hot fat. Serve cole slaw and an ice cream sundae of your choice for a homemade takeout meal.

3 pounds calamari
1 cup flour
Salt to taste
Oil for frying
Lemon wedges

Clean calamari (see instructions in Appetizers). Cut bodies into rings ½ inch wide. Separate tentacle clusters into two parts.

Spread flour in a pie plate or on wax paper and add salt to taste.

Have oil about 2 inches deep in an electric skillet and heat to 375° F. Dip rings in flour, shake off excess, and fry until lightly browned, about 2 minutes, turning to brown both sides. Do not crowd rings while frying; and if you have a spatter screen use it, as calamari sometimes bursts when frying. Remove with a slotted spoon or fork and drain on paper towels. Fried rings can be kept in a 200° F oven until all are fried. Serve with lemon wedges. Makes 4 servings.

Stuffed Calamari

A delicious addition to your cooking repertoire. Serve thin spaghetti with this dish if you wish.

2 pounds whole calamari (squid)

Stuffing

⅓ cup uncooked rice
½ cup finely chopped onion
¼ cup chopped green pepper
¼ cup chopped fresh parsley
¼ cup chopped linguica
½ teaspoon salt
Freshly ground pepper to taste
1 clove garlic, crushed
Chopped tentacles

(Stuffed Calamari continued)

Sauce

1 can (16 ounces) tomatoes
¾ cup dry white wine
½ cup chopped onion
½ teaspoon salt
Freshly ground pepper to taste
1 small jalapeno pepper, seeded and chopped
1 clove garlic, crushed

Clean calamari (see instructions in Appetizers). Soak in water while preparing stuffing.

Cook rice in 2 cups water for about 10 minutes. Drain. Combine with onion, green pepper, parsley, linguica, salt, pepper, garlic, and chopped tentacles. Mix lightly to blend. Drain calamari well and stuff loosely with rice mixture. Close open end with a toothpick or small skewer.

To make sauce combine remaining ingredients in a large saucepan. Bring to a boil and add stuffed calamari. Reduce heat, cover, and simmer, stirring occasionally, for 1 hour or until calamari are tender. Makes 4 servings.

New England Seafood Casserole

This casserole is one which I first ate years ago at Albert Stockli's restaurant in Ridgefield, Connecticut. It is a perfect casserole for entertaining as it can be fully prepared in advance, refrigerated, and baked when ready.

½ pound bay scallops
½ pound green shrimp
1 tablespoon butter
2 tablespoons finely chopped onion
¼ cup dry sherry
¼ cup clam juice
Salt and freshly ground pepper to taste
1 tablespoon lemon juice
1 teaspoon paprika
1 tablespoon Dijon style mustard
½ pound crabmeat
1½ teaspoons cornstarch
2 tablespoons water
2 egg yolks
2 tablespoons light cream
4 tablespoons mayonnaise

Wash scallops and remove any pieces of shell. Peel, devein, and wash shrimp.

Melt butter in a skillet and add scallops, shrimp, onion, sherry, clam juice, salt, pepper, and lemon juice. Stir in paprika and mustard. Reduce heat to medium and cook 5 minutes.

Remove scallops and shrimp to a shallow casserole and add crabmeat.

Dissolve cornstarch in water and add to liquid in skillet, cooking until thickened. Remove from heat. Beat egg yolks with cream and mayonnaise and fold into sauce. Pour over seafood in casserole.

If baking immediately, heat in a 400° F oven for 10 minutes or until bubbly and lightly browned.

If you prepare this dish in advance, cover lightly with wax paper or plastic wrap and refrigerate. Plan an extra 15 minutes for heating time.

Makes 4 to 6 servings.

Sauces

Sour Cream Tartar Sauce

Sour Cream Tartar sauce is a variation of Tartar Sauce, the standard sauce served with fried or broiled fish. It is a nice change, but we give you also the recipe for Tartar Sauce, below.

> 1 cup mayonnaise
> 2 tablespoons minced dill pickle
> 1 tablespoon minced onion
> 1 tablespoon lemon juice
> 1 tablespoon chopped fresh parsley
> 1 teaspoon each minced fresh tarragon, thyme, and dill
>   or ⅓ teaspoon each dried, crushed
> Freshly ground pepper to taste
> ¼ cup dairy sour cream

Combine mayonnaise with remaining ingredients except sour cream. Refrigerate. Just before serving, fold in sour cream. Makes about 1¼ cups.

Tartar Sauce

> 1 cup mayonnaise
> 2 tablespoons sweet pickle relish, drained
> 1 tablespoon minced onion
> 1 teaspoon chopped unsalted capers
> 1 tablespoon lemon juice

Mix all ingredients gently but thoroughly. Chill well. Makes about 1¼ cups. Will keep, covered, in refrigerator for several weeks.

Red Pepper Sauce for Fish

This and Horseradish Sauce (below) are delicious with plain broiled, baked, or fried fish.

1 medium red pepper
1 cup mayonnaise
1 green onion, chopped
1½ tablespoons finely chopped Spanish onion

Char pepper under broiler or over gas flame of burner. Remove skin with hands under cold running water. Remove core and seeds. Puree coarsely in a blender. Add to mayonnaise along with green onion and Spanish onion, mixing lightly. Chill. Refrigerate any leftover sauce. Makes 1¼ cups cups.

Horseradish Sauce for Fish

⅓ cup snipped fresh dill
1½ cups plain yogurt
⅓ cup prepared horseradish
2 teaspoons lemon juice

Combine all ingredients and mix lightly. Chill. Refrigerate any left-over sauce. Makes about 2 cups.

Flavored Butters

A piece of plain boiled, broiled, or steamed fish can often be made more flavorful with seasoned butter added to the fish after it is cooked. Here are a few that go well with fish. Serve at room temperature. Any seasoned butter that is left over may be refrigerated, but always bring to room temperature to serve.

Curry Butter

Mix 1 stick softened butter or margarine with 1½ tablespoons curry powder. Allow flavors to blend at room temperature for 1½ hours.

Lemon Butter

Mix 1 stick softened butter or margarine with 2 tablespoons fresh lemon juice. Allow flavors to blend at room temperature for 1½ hours. Variation: Add 1 tablespoon spicy prepared mustard with lemon juice.

Horseradish Butter

Mix 1 stick softened butter or margarine with 3 tablespoons drained prepared horseradish and 2 teaspoons lemon juice. Allow flavors to blend at room temperature for 1½ hours.

Barbecuing Fish

A hinged grill is almost a necessity for barbecuing fish. Fish steaks (such as swordfish, salmon, or cod) can be cooked right on the barbecue grill because the fish is thick enough so that it won't break apart. But even steak fish is more easily handled in a fish grill. A fish grill consists of two hinged rustproof wire racks with long handles. It is large enough to hold fish for six people. The grill is not expensive. (Fish grills are also useful for barbecuing chicken pieces, pork chops, or other small pieces of meat as well as fish.)

To use the grill, grease the racks well with oil, place the fish on one rack, and bring the other down over. Slip handle closure down so grill will not come open. Place on barbecue grill 3 to 4 inches above hot charcoal and cook fish the required length of time depending on its thickness. With the handles it is easy to turn the fish to cook both sides.

Don't be fooled into cooking the fish on aluminum foil. It has to get the flavor from the charcoal to be really barbecued.

* * *

Barbecued Fish, Italian

A nicely seasoned sauce flavors the fish.

2 pounds fish fillets (cod, haddock, ocean catfish, or
  other white-fleshed fish)
¼ cup olive oil
1 clove garlic, finely chopped
¼ cup finely chopped onion
2 tablespoons lemon juice
1 bay leaf
2 or 3 sprigs fresh thyme or ⅛ teaspoon ground thyme
Freshly ground pepper to taste
1 can (8 ounces) tomato sauce
¼ cup water
2 or 3 sprigs parsley, chopped

Place fish fillets in a flat pan. In a skillet or small saucepan, heat oil
and saute garlic and onion over medium heat for 5 minutes. Add remaining ingredients and simmer for 5 minutes. Pour about two-thirds
of hot sauce over fish in pan. Refrigerate for 30 minutes to 2 hours.

When ready to cook, place fish fillets in an oiled fish grill. Cook over
hot charcoal about 4 inches from source of heat for about 10 minutes,
basting with sauce. Turn to brown both sides. When fish flakes easily
with fork, serve with leftover sauce. Makes 4 servings.

Herbed Lemon Barbecued Fish

A flavorful marinade adds to the taste of the fish. Serve potato salad, corn on the cob, hot bread, garden lettuce with oil and vinegar, and watermelon with the barbecued fish.

> 2 pounds fish fillets (ocean catfish, tautog, or bluefish)
> ½ cup salad oil
> 1 teaspoon freshly grated lemon peel
> ⅓ cup fresh lemon juice
> ¼ cup minced onion
> ¼ teaspoon salt
> Freshly ground pepper to taste
> ¼ teaspoon dried rosemary leaves, crushed
> ¼ teaspoon dried thyme leaves, crushed
> 2 tablespoons chopped fresh parsley

Place fish fillets in a flat dish.

Combine salad oil with remaining ingredients and pour over fish. Cover and marinate for 2 hours or overnight in the refrigerator, turning occasionally. Remove fish from marinade and place in a greased fish grill.

Grill 4 inches from hot coals about 10 minutes, depending on thickness of fillets, turning once. Baste two or three times with marinade during cooking. Makes 4 servings.

Barbecued Fish Fillets Creole

One of the great things about barbecues is that so much of the preparation can be done hours in advance. To serve with Barbecued Fish Fillets Creole plan a snappy macaroni salad. Take advantage of the season and have lots of corn on the cob and plenty of hot bread for hungry outdoor appetites. Make dessert easy by serving ripe nectarines or peaches and cheese.

1 small onion, chopped
1 clove garlic, crushed
2 tablespoons butter or margarine
1 tablespoon cornstarch
1½ cups water
2 tablespoons white vinegar
1 tablespoon lemon juice
1 tablespoon soy sauce
2 teaspoons brown sugar
Freshly ground pepper to taste
½ cup catsup
2 teaspoons Worcestershire sauce
½ teaspoon dry mustard
2 pounds boneless fish fillets (cod, haddock, or hake)

Lightly brown onion and garlic in butter. Mix cornstarch with water and add to onion mixture. Bring to a boil, stirring. Add remaining ingredients except fish. Cool to room temperature. Put fish fillets in a flat dish. Add enough sauce to cover fish and marinate in refrigerator at least 2 hours, turning several times.

Place fillets in a well-greased fish grill. Grill 4 inches from hot coals 8 to 10 minutes, depending on thickness of fillets, or until fish flakes easily with a fork. Turn once and baste with sauce during cooking. Heat any leftover sauce and serve with grilled fish. Makes 4 servings.

Tom's Grilled Stuffed Flounder

This is such a good recipe you'll be glad you've invested in a fish grill. You might make a tasty rice salad, lightly steamed zucchini, rye bread and butter sandwiches, and cantaloupe for dessert to serve with it.

2 pounds flounder fillets
¼ cup finely chopped onion
2 tablespoons vegetable oil
1 slice white bread
2 tablespoons brandy
1 tablespoon chopped fresh basil or 1 teaspoon dried, crushed
2 or 3 sprigs fresh thyme or ⅛ teaspoon ground
½ teaspoon salt
Freshly ground pepper to taste
2 long slices natural Swiss cheese
Softened butter or margarine

You need four 8-inch-long fillets about 4 inches wide. If you do not have four large fillets, combine smaller pieces. They can be held together with a small skewer or toothpicks. Place flat on a piece of wax paper. Trim off end pieces to square fillets. There should be at least ½ cup of end pieces, but if you have more, use them all.

Saute onion in oil until tender but not browned. Add end pieces from fillets and cook several minutes until fish can be flaked. Crumble bread into skillet. Add brandy and seasonings and stir until well blended. Spoon about 2 tablespoons of the mixture down center of each fillet. Cut Swiss cheese slices in half lengthwise and place on filling. Roll fillets, starting at narrow end. If cheese wants to peek out, bend slice back so it is covered by fish. Place stuffed fillets in an oiled fish grill. (You cannot do this dish without a grill.) Spread fillets with softened butter. Grill 3 to 4 inches from hot charcoal for about 15 minutes, turning to cook both sides. Remove any toothpicks or skewers before serving. Makes 4 servings.

Portuguese Grilled Fish

This is a spicy marinade to give the fish real flavor. If using French bread, split lengthwise and butter. Cut crosswise into lengths to fit fish.

 2 cloves garlic, crushed
 ½ teaspoon crushed red pepper
 1 teaspoon paprika
 1 teaspoon salt
 2 bay leaves, cut up
 1 cup wine vinegar
 2 cups water
 2 pounds boneless fish fillets (pollock, cod, or hake)
 8 frankfurter rolls or French bread

Combine seasonings with vinegar and water in a large stainless steel or glass bowl. Add fish and marinate overnight in refrigerator, turning now and then.

When ready to cook, cut fish into strips about 1½ inches wide and 6 inches long and put onto oiled fish grill. Close grill and cook about 4 inches above hot charcoal. Turn and brush with marinade while cooking, which takes about 10 minutes. Serve in buttered rolls or French bread. Makes 8 servings.

Marinade for Salmon or Swordfish Kabobs

Many fish markets sell small pieces of swordfish and salmon at lower prices than the steak-cut size. These pieces are excellent to skewer for barbecuing. They can be barbecued by themselves, or the pieces of fish may be alternated with green pepper squares, small parboiled onions, mushrooms, cherry tomatoes, zucchini squash chunks, or other vegetables of your choice.

 1 can (8 ounces) tomato sauce
 ¼ cup lemon juice
 2 tablespoons honey
 2 tablespoons finely chopped onion
 Dash Tabasco sauce
 ¼ cup oil
 Salmon or swordfish cubes

Mix all ingredients except fish in a bowl. Add fish; marinate for several hours in the refrigerator. Put fish on skewers and grill 3 to 4 inches from hot charcoal until fish flakes easily, turning during cooking. This should take 8 to 10 minutes depending on size of fish cubes. Makes about 1½ cups marinade, enough for about 1½ pounds fish.

Grilled Salmon with Dill Sauce

Dill and salmon make exemplary partners in this simple recipe.

2 pounds salmon steaks, ¾ inch thick
Salt and freshly ground pepper to taste
2 tablespoons oil (or more if needed)
4 tablespoons butter or margarine
4 tablespoons chopped fresh dill

Rub salmon steaks with salt, pepper, and oil. Place in fish grill. Broil about 4 inches from hot charcoal, about 10 minutes on each side.

While salmon is grilling, heat together butter and dill. Serve hot with grilled salmon. Makes 4 servings.

Vegetable Kabobs

When planning a barbecue, consider vegetable kabobs as part of the meal. Chunks of zucchini or green pepper, cherry tomatoes, summer squash, or small parboiled onions can be put on skewers, brushed lightly with oil, and barbecued over the charcoal. Begin after the fish has been turned and grill the vegetables 10 minutes, turning. This makes a good accompaniment to any barbecued plain fish.

Blue Special

Bluefish is so abundant on the Cape in the summer that it would be a shame not to use it. This good recipe for grilling should appeal to everyone.

> 2 pounds boneless bluefish fillets
> 2 teaspoons mustard seed
> 2 teaspoons Dijon style mustard
> 1 clove garlic
> 2 teaspoons (about) coarsely cracked peppercorns
> 3 tablespoons lemon juice

Place bluefish fillets skin side down in a flat pan. In a mortar and pestle crush mustard seed with mustard and garlic until blended. Stir in cracked pepper to taste. Spread over fish fillets and sprinkle with lemon juice. Let stand in refrigerator for several hours before grilling. Place in oiled fish grill and put fish 3 to 4 inches above hot coals. Grill for 8 minutes or until fish flakes. Makes 4 servings.

Tangy Barbecue Sauce

Another marinade for broiled or barbecued bluefish.

> ½ cup lemon juice
> ⅓ cup oil
> 1 tablespoon minced onion
> Dash Tabasco sauce
> 1 teaspoon fresh thyme or ⅓ teaspoon dried

Combine all ingredients and pour over fish. Let marinate in refrigerator for several hours. Enough for 1½ to 2 pounds bluefish.

Brother Girard's Grilled Scallops and Bacon

Skewered scallops and bacon make a fine barbecued dish. The ingredients can be prepared and skewered in advance and refrigerated until ready to bring to the charcoal grill.

1 pound ocean scallops
¼ cup honey
¼ cup soy sauce
¼ cup lemon juice
8 slices bacon
4 cherry tomatoes

Wash scallops and remove any pieces of shell. Drain. Combine honey, soy sauce, and lemon juice in a flat pan. Add scallops and marinate in refrigerator about 2 hours, turning scallops with a spoon now and then.

Cook bacon slices until partially done. Remove scallops from marinade. Put scallops on skewers, stringing bacon between and around scallops. Top each skewer with tomato. Grill 3 to 4 inches from hot charcoal for about 8 minutes, turning. Baste with marinade while cooking. Makes 4 servings.

Grilled Whole Fish

A whole fish cooked on the outdoor charcoal grill can be a spectacular main dish for a meal. Any whole fish that does not hang off the grill can be barbecued.

Gut the fish, wash well, and dry. Leave the head on or cut it off as you prefer. The fish can be cooked in the round or split. Either way, it is best to secure the fish in a fish grill to make it easy to turn when the time comes.

The fish in the round can be filled with fresh or dried herbs such as tarragon, dill, thyme, or parsley.

Or herbs can be tossed on the gray coals when you are ready to add the fish for cooking. The trendy flavoring is mesquite added to the coals, which gives the fish a pleasant flavor.

Place fish about 4 inches above hot coals. A fish weighing 5 to 6 pounds will take 20 to 45 minutes, being turned once during the cooking time. Baste fish with a mixture of lemon juice and melted butter. Test fish with knife point to see that the fish flakes easily.

Some fish that are good to grill whole are small cod, salmon, bluefish, trout, whitefish, or flounder. Even smelt and herring can be grilled, though they will cook much more quickly than their larger counterparts.

Barbecue Marinades

Marinade for Cod or Haddock

¾ cup red wine vinegar
½ cup dry white wine
2 teaspoons Worcestershire sauce
¼ teaspoon dried marjoram leaves, crushed

Combine all ingredients. Pour over fish in a stainless steel or glass dish and refrigerate for 1 hour or longer, turning fish several times. This is enough for 1½ to 2 pounds fish.

Marinade for Swordfish or Salmon

1 cup oil
⅓ cup fresh lemon juice
2 green onions, sliced thinly
1 tablespoon chopped fresh tarragon or 1 teaspoon
    dried, crushed
2 teaspoons Dijon style mustard
Freshly ground pepper to taste

Combine all ingredients and use as a marinade for swordfish, Mako shark, or salmon. Marinate fish for several hours in refrigerator and baste with marinade during grilling. Makes enough for 2 or 3 pounds of fish.

Tropical Marinade

2 tablespoons oil
1 cup orange juice
¼ cup sugar
¼ cup cidar vinegar
2 tablespoons lemon juice
3 tablespoons soy sauce

Combine all ingredients, stirring to dissolve sugar. Pour over fish in pan and marinate in refrigerator for several hours, turning fish now and then. When grilling fish baste with marinade. This is enough marinade for about 2 pounds fish. Use for white-fleshed fish, bluefish, or mackerel.

Preserving
Seafood

· FREEZING ·

Freeze Cape Cod seafood at home to retain that wonderful fresh taste for future eating. Always freeze fish as quickly as possible after buying or catching. Freezing only preserves what you have, it does not enhance it.

To freeze is to store properly wrapped food at 0° F or lower. A freezer can be a separate piece of equipment or part of your refrigerator. If the latter, it should be isolated from the refrigerator section with a dividing wall and have either a separate outside door or an insulated inner door. Many ice cube compartments are intended only for short storage, not long-term freezing — so check to be certain.

Proper freezer packaging keeps air from the food and protects it so it is clean and sanitary. Packaging can be plastic film or bags, laminated paper, aluminum freezer foil, plastic or paperboard containers, or straight-sided glass containers. Packages should be sealed with freezer tape, masking tape, or metal twists. Heat sealing devices are also available. All food packages should be labeled and dated with a marking pencil.

Freezer storage time of seafood is 4 to 6 months. Seafood should always, ideally, be defrosted in the refrigerator. It is important to defrost seafood completely before cooking. Partly frozen seafood will throw off the length of cooking time and make it difficult for you to achieve optimum results.

* * *

Freezing Fish Fillets

Because fish is perishable and its flavor changes quickly, keep it iced while transporting it from where it is caught or bought to home, if any distance is involved.

Fish fillets can be wrapped separately, frozen, then stored in a freezer bag or box to keep them together in one package. To freeze fillets in one package, separate them with plastic wrap for easier defrosting.

Rinse fillets and pat dry. Lay each fillet in center of a piece of freezer wrap. Bring wrap up around fish tightly so air is squeezed out. Seal with freezer tape and mark variety of fish and date frozen.

Freezing Whole Fish and Steaks

Whole fish should be scaled, gutted, washed, dried, and frozen without head. Stuff the gutted belly with aluminum foil crumpled to fit. It will help to defrost the fish a little more quickly when you are ready to cook it. Wrap, seal, and label.

Fish steaks should be wrapped separately and then overwrapped or bagged together. This gives two advantages. First, the steaks are easily separated for faster defrosting; second, if you want only one or two steaks at a time individual wrapping makes that possible.

Freezing Clams, Scallops, Lobster, Shrimp

Many people freeze clams, scallops, lobster, and particularly shrimp in the shell. There is nothing wrong with this if you have sufficient freezer space to accommodate the extra bulk of the shells. Scrub clam and scallop shells well, rinse, and dry before freezing. Put into freezer bags so they will be contained and protected from freezer burn. Lobster should be cooked before freezing. Wash outer shell and dry. Shrimp can be cooked or green, and should also be washed and dried. Both lobster and shrimp should be packed in freezer bags, and all packages should be labeled and dated.

Lobster meat may have a tendency to become slightly watery when defrosted. You can squeeze the lobster to remove the liquid before using it in a recipe. If the recipe calls for any liquid, use the juice you squeezed from the lobster.

Shucked scallops should be frozen in packages the appropriate size for your usual needs.

To freeze clam meat, open shells (see instructions in Chowders and Soups) and cut clam free from shell. Some people insist that the stomach be removed, others freeze the whole clam. Yours is the choice. If the clams are to be used primarily for chowder, chop them before freezing and freeze juice separately. Freeze in containers or bags that suit your recipe size.

And I can't emphasize enough to label and date everything. Once a package gets into the freezer and is frozen, it seems to take on a new identity unless it is named.

· PICKLING ·

Pickled seafood is treated with a mixture of vinegar, sugar, and spices. Most of us are familiar with commercially pickled herring or whitefish. At home you can pickle almost any of our Massachusetts fish. As with any fish preservation, always use truly fresh fish.

*   *   *

Pickled Fish

5 pounds fish, cut in 2- to 3-inch pieces
½ tablespoon whole allspice and ½ tablespoon mustard
   seed, *or* 1 tablespoon regular mixed pickling spice
2 cups sliced onion
2 or 3 bay leaves
1 quart white vinegar
2¼ cups water
½ tablespoon white pepper
½ teaspoon ground red pepper
1 cup (about) sliced onion

Soak the fish in a weak brine — 1 cup noniodized salt to 1 gallon (4 quarts) cold water — for 1 hour. After its brine soaking, rinse the fish in fresh water.

Combine all remaining ingredients except the 1 cup sliced onion in a large saucepan. Bring to a boil and add the fish. Simmer for about 10 minutes or until fish can be flaked easily with a fork. Remove fish from liquid and place in a single layer in a flat pan. Refrigerate for rapid cooling. Then pack cold fish in clean glass canning jars, adding a few of the spices from the pickling liquid and some freshly sliced onion to each jar. Strain pickling solution, bring to a boil and pour over fish in jars. Seal with new 2-part lids at once. Store in the refrigerator. Must be used within 4 to 6 weeks. Makes 5 to 6 pints.

Pickled Oysters or Mussels

These pickled oysters or mussels make a first course that is different or can be used as hors d'oeuvres. Serve with sour cream.

50 shelled oysters (about 2½ pints) or about 2½ pounds mussels
1 teaspoon noniodized salt
1 cup white vinegar
12 peppercorns
12 cloves
2 bay leaves
¼ teaspoon ground red pepper

To pickle oysters: Put oysters, including liquor, in a glass, enamel, or stainless steel pan. Add salt and bring slowly to scalding point. Do not boil, and remove from heat before oysters' edges curl. Cool.

To pickle mussels: Clean and steam in ¼ cup water just long enough to open. Reserve broth. Remove mussels from shell as soon as cool enough to handle. Put mussels and broth in a glass, enamel, or stainless steel pan. Add salt and bring to boiling point. Remove mussels and cool.

Strain cooking liquid and return it to pan. Add vinegar and seasonings to liquid, bring to boiling point, and pour over oysters or mussels. Cover and refrigerate. Let marinate 1 or 2 days in refrigerator and serve as an hors d'oeuvre or first course. Makes about 2 pints.

Bob's Smelts in Tomato Pickling Sauce

In a recipe such as Bob's Smelts in Tomato Pickling Sauce, the size of the smelts determines how much sauce is needed. Since this recipe makes about 2 cups of sauce, the 16 smelts recommended here should be fairly small.

½ cup oil
½ cup vinegar (cider or white)
¼ cup water
½ cup catsup
3 tablespoons sugar
¼ teaspoon salt
1 teaspoon pickling spice
6 peppercorns
16 smelts (or fewer, depending on size)

Combine oil, vinegar, water, catsup, and seasonings. Bring to a boil and simmer several minutes. Gut smelts, remove heads, and wash well. Add to pickling sauce and simmer slowly for 10 minutes. Be sure fish is covered by pickling sauce. Refrigerate 18 to 24 hours in sauce before serving.

· SMOKING ·

Smoke only fresh fish in order for it to have the very best flavor. The fish can be filleted, steaked, whole, or split. If whole the fish should be scaled and gutted. Split fish should be cut just to the back and opened flat. Eel smokes well also. For successful smoking try to smoke pieces of fish that are as near the same size and thickness as possible at one time.

* * *

Equipment for Smoking

You can buy commerically made smokers; you can use a covered barbecue grill as a smoker; or you can make a smoker from a metal drum or wooden barrel. The fish is put on a wire screen hung on dowels or laid on slats at the top of the smoker, and the smoke fire is at the bottom of the smoker.

To make a metal drum smoker: Use a cleaned 50-gallon oil or alcohol drum. Use a chisel or torch to cut out the top of the drum. Cut about 3 inches off this lid all around, and suspend it from 3 brackets 13 inches from the open top end of the drum to make a heat baffle. Cut out a section of the drum near the bottom for a fire pit door. A door may be made from lightweight metal on a single hinge. Use heavy wire mesh to make a tray to hold fish and suspend it 3 inches from top by wire brackets. The smoker may covered with a wooden or metal lid.

Heat and Smoke Source

For an improvised smoker an iron skillet on an electric hot plate does very nicely. Sawdust or wood chips placed in the skillet are lighted and allowed to smolder. Or burn charcoal in a grill to a light gray ash, then sprinkle on wet wood chips or sawdust to make smoke.

Oak, apple, ash, hickory, or maple wood chips are used for smoke. If you have old apple trees with falling branches, apple is supposed to be one of the best woods for smoking. Resin-containing woods such as pine should be avoided.

Brining and Smoking Procedures

Before fish is smoked it must be brined. A mixture of 1½ cups salt and 1 gallon (4 quarts) cold water is enough brine for 4 pounds of fish. Use a glass, enamel, or heavy plastic container and let the fish soak in the brine at 40° F (refrigerature temperature) for at least 12 hours.

When ready to smoke, remove fish from brine, drain, wash well, and air dry for about 30 minutes. Place fish skin side down on wire rack or dowels. The air temperature in the smoker should be about 100° F when smoking starts. For best results use a short-stemmed metal meat thermometer to check temperature of fish as it is smoked. Insert thermometer into thickest part of fish, tying it in place if necessary. During smoking the temperature inside the smoker should rise to 225° F. The fish should reach 180° F and stay this temperature for 30 minutes. This cooks the fish and stops bacterial growth. The whole process in the smoker takes about 4 hours.

These are basic directions for smoking. Once you become familiar with the basics you may like to experiment by adding spices to the brine, using different kinds of wood to get different smoke flavors, or smoking longer than 4 hours to get a smokier fish.

If you have a commercial smoker, follow the directions that come with it as to amount of charcoal for length of smoking time. The fish should be brined or marinated before smoking. A brine made of 1 quart water with ¼ cup salt is enough for 2 to 3 pounds fish fillets. Let fillets soak, covered, in refrigerator for several hours or overnight. Before starting the smoking, wash fish well and let air dry for 30 minutes.

For additional flavor add 1 tablespoon dried tarragon to water pan; or if your smoker does not have a water pan, add tarragon to brine.

You may also marinate, instead of brining. A good marinade is 1 cup dry white wine with ¼ cup each soy sauce and lemon juice.

Or for further flavor, brush brined or marinated fish with your favorite barbecue sauce before smoking. Smoke 2 to 3 hours.

For smoked shrimp, lobster, oysters, or mussels, marinate in lemon juice and your favorite Italian dressing for several hours. Smoke for 1 or 2 hours. If shrimp, oysters, or mussels are too small for rack, make a tray of aluminum foil, butter it well, and poke a few holes in it. Place on rack and put shrimp, oysters, or mussels on tray.

Fish smoked for 4 hours according to the basic directions above may be stored, wrapped, in the refrigerator, but should be used within a month. Or it can be wrapped and frozen and will keep 4 months at 0° F.

I use a commercial smoker, not being clever enough to make one, and the fish is smoked fairly quickly over steam. I use apple and maple chips over charcoal. The time required does not smoke the fish enough for refrigerator storage as long as a month. I can keep my smoked fish in the refrigerator for a week, or freeze it for up to 4 months.

Index